AF521628

The Struggle

Marie Pepsin

Baltimore, Maryland

The Struggle

Library of Congress
Cataloging-in-Publication Data
ISBN 1-56167-783-3

Library of Congress Card Catalog Number:
2003092456

illustrations by Marie Pepsin

Published by

8019 Belair Road, Suite 10
Baltimore, Maryland 21236

Manufactured in the United States of America

Table of Contents

PREFACE

For a long time, I have read, studied and am now being led by the Holy Spirit to write this book. He wishes to convey love... and as I write of the struggle that is taking place in so many lives, you will feel the hand of God in all that is happening.

This book must be a book that will relate to many who read it, possibly to help in any struggle that is taking place, as God's word states so clearly that this would be happening. In many instances you will detect the human element of interpreting many events as they were conveyed to the author. The people involved may have wanted an entirely different message conveyed, but to the author, it was taken in light of her own interpretation. Consequently, the names of people involved have been changed or left out, to protect their identity and also to establish an outlook of the author, not to cause any controversy. Hopefully, you will be a part of this book, yet after reading it, you will feel joy, peace and victory.

Before I continue any further, I bind any evil spirit, in the precious name of Jesus Christ and by the power of His precious blood, who is keeping anyone in bondage from getting to our Lord and Savior, Jesus Christ, in a personal way. All the intellectual knowledge and historical knowledge, will not do anyone any good, unless you allow Jesus to enter your heart and to know he is alive and ministering to us daily. When doing so, John 1:12 states, "But as many as received Him, to them He gave power to become the Sons of God."

Parents, no matter how much money you spend on educating your child or children, no matter how much material things you give them, nothing will mean a thing. The important thing you can do for your children is to tell them of the plan of salvation through Jesus Christ and about getting to know Him in a personal way. They will respect you beyond belief, even if at first they do reject it, but do plant the seed and keep watering it.

The Struggle

Jesus said, "I am the way, the truth, and the life: no man cometh unto the Father, but by me." (John 14:6). There is one God and one mediator between God and man, the man, Jesus Christ (Timothy 2:5,6). "Neither is there salvation in any other: for there is none other name under heaven given among men, whereby we must be saved." (Acts 4:12).

Already the STRUGGLE is going on in so many hearts and minds whether to believe the Bible or go as the self thinks it should. Some people pick and choose when and if it suits their way. They point to the Bible when they want to bring out a point, and if the Bible again then speaks against any of what they are doing, that it is not in accord to His word, they then say, "Oh, the Bible was written by mere men who err." Or that "it was written so long ago!" God does not change; His word is for today. Jesus came to show us the way and how to love. The self or conscience area can be a playground of Satan himself. So as I write, I pray for you to allow the Holy Spirit into your heart, allowing your faith to open doors that you never dreamed possible. Allowing Him to lead and guide and be Lord of your life, not conscience. Go one level beyond that, into the spirit. But before you open the door, accept Jesus Christ as your Lord and Savior; accept that He died for your sins to be truly under the blood. Then open the door to your everything!

By faith, not by sight, it is by faith through grace that we are saved. Allow this spark of new awareness to become a reality. It is the only way it works! God is the center of our lives and we must accept His graciousness and the gift of His Holy Spirit. By His Holy Cross, thou shall renew the face of the earth!

If for any reason the human element projects more so than the Spirit, I ask you to read, but allow the criticism being offered to be gentle, humble, and constructive. Hopefully there will be no condemnation, for the Holy Spirit doesn't condemn. Oh the words of a beautiful child, "He meets you right where you are, accepts you for what you are, and then gently leads and guides you, bringing you to the fullness of what He created you to be."

The greatest struggle is the comforting of a child who is trying to establish himself in the ways of God in such a complex world. To enjoy the peace and joy of the Lord Jesus Christ while so many in the body of Christ are battling each other. Even the elect are being deceived.

This is a book to meditate on, to put oneself into and to express your views as it confirms with your spirit. In spite of the struggle, abuses, ridiculing, judgments, persecution, and seeming death, always allow His love to shine forth. Therein lies the victory.

FOREWORD

As the story unfolds, one can detect and pick out the forces and the struggles involved: the forces at work, people forces, negative, positive, good, evil, ego forces, etc., etc. However, the force of the Holy Spirit just radiates beautifully, joyously and without reservation.

To be able to put yourself into this book is the most rewarding, for without YOU, this means nothing. We are all part of God, in the name of Jesus Christ.

A positive force enters in when the first chapter is tested on a twelve-year-old daughter, Jessica. She inspires the writer by making the statement, "That is great, mom! Whenever anyone talks about Jesus Christ, I get tingly all over. I just loved the first chapter!"

I shall not test it on any adult. You, yourself, will be the positive or negative force. A child shall lead me; she, too, being led by the Holy Spirit.

Forces of denominations are entering in...revealing many facets there: the terrible struggle of trying to disregard all the experiences there; to disregard men in authority not being born again and therefore unable to be under their submission and then becoming so totally absorbed in Jesus Christ and the leading of the Holy Spirit; the struggle to have your people understand, when you yourself don't quite understand fully, why the Lord put you in these situations, such as the one you were in...in many areas, in time. The ultimate end result was to bring the true message of Jesus Christ and what it meant to be BORN AGAIN, to lead the people back to the Bible and the salvation of their souls.

In loving and caring, plus having great concern for each other, is leading us into this story. We are all in this world, yet not of this world, waiting the arrival of our precious Savior, THE LORD JESUS CHRIST, to come and take us with Him to the place He has gone and prepared for us. Jesus Christ, the Divine Son of God, leads us through the Bible, with His now and ever present Holy Spirit, is still leading us through His Word. Leading us to His Second Coming, bringing His people to perfection. Bringing His people out of bondage, out of the world and back to the Bible...His Word, His World.

Alpha and omega (beginning and the end), the end of this era into the beginning of the light, we wait for a place He had gone to prepare for us.

Read the words of Jesus himself: "Let not your heart be troubled: ye believe in God, believe also in me. In my Father's house are many mansions: if it were not so, I would have told you. I go to prepare a place for you. And if I go and prepare a place for you, I WILL COME AGAIN, and receive you unto myself; that where I am, there ye may be also." (John 14: 1,3).

This is a promise made by Jesus. Stand firm on His promise. He is not a God to lie. He will come again for His children.

Jesus was taken up into heaven forty days after His resurrection. The disciples saw Him disappear in a cloud. This same Jesus, who was taken from you into heaven, shall come in like manner as you saw Him go into heaven (Acts 1:10, 11).

The revelation, at which time, every eye shall see him (Revelation 1:7).

FALSE CHRISTS
ENERGY
HYPNOSIS
E.S.P.
PEOPLE
FORCES
UNDER THE COVERING OF JESUS CHRIST
EYES ON CHRIST!
GIFTS OF THE HOLY SPIRIT
THE WAY
JESUS
ALL KINDS OF PHILOPHIE TRYING TO BE FED IN
VIBRATIONS
THE PIT
COLORS
DENOMINATIONS
RELIGIONS
THE STRUGGLE

Introduction

This is the great adventure of a woman's involvement with a pilgrim church, the Roman Catholic Church, coming through the gates of tradition, searching and seeking to understand the gifts of the Holy Spirit, having already had some experience in them. It is about knowing the historical Jesus Christ, our Lord and Savior, and then slowly coming to have a very personal relationship through the Baptism of the Holy Spirit. It is about being filled with the Holy Spirit and then encountering the counterfeit, the disappointments, and heartache of her own church members not understanding the mission that God has led her into, and that is... working to save the lost suffering souls. Then there was also Satan's attacks on her daughter. Satan, who was unable to penetrate into her life, tries to get at her through her daughter whom she loved very, very much. However, it was such a wonderful victory that emerged by her spiritual awareness of what was happening. To be alert and spiritually aware of the gentle leading of the Holy Spirit brought the peace and joy of really knowing that she was truly a child of God.

At the same time having the joy and support of the true born again believers who were also spirit filled through their personal relationship with Jesus Christ as Lord and Savior. The true glory and praise belongs only to Jesus, in its entirety, for it was only through Him that He only fully understood the mission that the author was given.

While encountering many diversified Christian groups, with whom to pray, study and feed on the word of God, it gave her the support and strength she so badly needed on this type of mission. This all could not have been done alone. She desperately needed the support of true, born again believers. Being in enemy territory, to rescue certain people from the clutches of Satan was not easy.

The Struggle

After drawing several people out of the terrible clutches of Satan, telling them about Jesus and the scriptures, they were saved through the blood of Jesus Christ. Many are still blinded and have not yet come into the fullness; however, much prayer is going up for them. Somewhere, sometime, I pray to God that He will lead them to a deliverance service.

In spite of all the obstacles and struggles, the woman finally flowers out into the person that God created her to be and to receive all that God has for her. Life abundant! Life eternal through Jesus Christ! Jesus is the only way!

It is to share this wonderful experience of all the forces that are at work in our lives, and to get total victory through Jesus Christ. He is Lord and still is on the throne. He is alive, and no matter what, He is still in control. The focus is on Jesus Christ, not on any traditional, excessive formality bogging down the movement of the Holy Spirit. The weeds have to go so that the flowering can take hold to blossom to the fullest! Praise God! Jesus Christ is Lord!

The Struggle is an arresting, original work that persuades any reader that the power of faith can help overcome his problems. At the heart of Marie C. Pepsin's book is the concept that faith and love for one's fellow man can conquer adversity. Recommended for publication for its unique subject matter, lucid explanation of a difficult subject, and the importance of this point of view.

Chapter I
The Struggle Begins

Already the forces are at work, negative advice... "You, write a book? You are not qualified!" But something greater that is in me said, "DO IT. WRITE IT!" Even prior to sitting down at my typewriter, feelings of "oh, forget it, it will be too much of a hassle" were there. There are days of so much distraction keeping me very occupied. Forces that I know do not want me to write this book nor get it in print. There are feelings of just wasting my precious time and your time, if you decide to read it. As I pray for the leading of the Holy Spirit, I know I am compelled to begin, for without His help, this would be impossible.

These forces are at work constantly as I begin. The phone is ringing, people are setting up appointments, etc., but in the midst of all of this, I manage to be a witness for Jesus Christ. Yet, there are some good, positive distractions used for the glory of God, so really it was not a waste of time to turn it over to Jesus, even though in the beginning it was to run me off course. There is victory in this way.

How important it is to have the discernment to deal with that which is of God, or for God. There are so many distractions. Be aware of the difference.

The struggle on the part of those who have opened their hearts to Jesus Christ, to have a personal relationship with Him and having come into the fullness of the Spirit...it is so beautiful to see. To see and feel their concern for the salvation of their fellow men. To lead others into the realization that Jesus Christ is the way, the truth and the life. There is no other name under heaven given among men, whereby we must be saved. (Acts 4:12) He is the only Savior. Believe on the Lord Jesus Christ, and thou shall be saved. (Acts 16:31)

The Struggle

We are all part of this book, so as you read, put yourself into it. The true beauty of committing your life to Jesus Christ is the most exciting life anyone can have. Each day brings a new adventure, along with a regular job, that goes along with our earthly life. We do have our responsibilities here in the earthly life, but each day, we must be ready to bring the message of Jesus through wisdom, to be applied to this life.

There are so many distractions that do take us off into other areas of literature and man's philosophy, which still give advice, but what we desperately need is the word of God. In dealing with the world, we must never take our eyes off Jesus Christ. "Oh, the joy that fills my heart," knowing He is always with me and will never forsake me. The realization...it is only you, yourself, that shuts Him out. Open your heart and let Jesus in. "Oh, the joy that floods my soul."

As I wait in earnest for direction, knowing within myself this is a story, I wonder how important it is to do away with the ego self; put the ego self aside and have the anointing of the Holy Spirit that this book will be written. Many of you are struggling and searching for the truth. One consolation is that one cannot suppress the truth. The Spirit is moving all over. This is what was spoken through the prophet Joel: "And it shall come to pass in the last days, says the Lord, that I will pour forth of my Spirit upon all flesh; and your sons and your daughters shall prophesy, and your young men shall see visions, and your old men shall dream dreams. And moreover upon my servants and upon my handmaids in those days will I pour forth of my spirit and they shall prophesy." (Acts 2: 16-19)

How great thou Art! One cannot help but to sing when one has the truth. We can face tomorrow. Parts of songs just flow through my mind. Happiness! Remember that song title? Also, Jesus is Lord. ALLELUIA! KING OF KINGS!

Even if the day is dull, drab and raining, and the color is also gray. What a wonderful time it is to pray and read your Bible. It is prayer that warms the heart, brings in the light, clears the air and stimulates action. It is putting oil in your lamp. The day becomes bright inside, even though it looks gray outside. Praise the Lord! The negative force tends to concentrate on the terrible day it is outside. Everyday is the day of the Lord and be glad He is. Happy is the day when the Lord will lead me in directions I never thought of. How wonderful it is to put yourself in His hands. What a wonderful, exciting adventure!

The struggle again begins to be able to stay at my typewriter or to find an answer for a friend in need, for she too needs ministering. Already the Holy Spirit has led me to a book where I will find the answer. So that was taken care of, when all of a sudden the phone starts to ring again. I now find myself in all directions, but upon lifting this all up to Jesus, I am lead by discerning that I should continue here at my typewriter, for it is no emergency, I just know it. When the Holy Spirit moves, be obedient to Him; do not quench the Spirit.

Before I sat down to write this book, I had an altogether different format to follow. The Holy Spirit has taken over and led me entirely into other areas. As he leads, the story unfolds gradually in its time and place.

It is all so important to know what is happening to the NOW, prior to writing this book. Here I am, with all of the uncertainty of what will happen with this story. Will I send it to a publisher? Or just let it hang around? Throw it in the wastebasket or even burn it in the fireplace? Really, there are forces at work, which I shall say are negative at this moment. For something that is greater in me says, "This book is going to be terrific!" So prepare the way, ALLELUIA!

Having a close walk with Jesus Christ, yet not having come into the fullness of the Holy Spirit, yet at a high point, I realize that things of a supernatural nature are taking place in my life. Knowing the gifts of the Holy Spirit do exist, I venture out to learn more about them. The forces at once begin to work, leading me into different areas of learning. Having a love for humanity, I venture into the learning process, under the direction of the Holy Spirit. With the gift of discernment yet uncertain, the great struggle begins. Every so often, questions begin to arise: Why am I in this situation? Does God want me here? Does He have a ministry and service for me to render? He leads me into a situation, teaching me by hearing, seeing, feeling, smelling, touching and expressing myself, in the name of Jesus Christ. Leading me into situations, perhaps that were not of Him, but the other forces entering in. However, sometimes being led in and then, soon led out of a certain particular situation, thus realizing it was by the presence of the Holy Spirit. At certain times, I would remain for awhile, only to find myself being of service to Him. People there needed to be ministered to, to hear about Jesus Christ, our Lord and Savior.

While in the learning process, I would start to get muddled up some. But the Holy Spirit would immediately send His other servants to clarify things, particularly through a girl named Jerry and some young and older men. One was named Michael, one named John, and another named Neil. Praise God for these fine spirit-filled, dedicated men!

The greatest light bearer, teacher and son, leader, soul winner, musician, comforter, and strength was John, my dear son. Praise God for John!

It was through these people that I was led into the fullness of the Holy Spirit, through Holy Scripture, shown plainly the word of God. Most of all it was through God's grace. For no one can save yourself. The Bible states, "By the grace you are saved through faith: and not of yourselves: it is the gift of God: not by works, lest any man should boast." (Ephesians 2:8,9).

After the struggle of seeking answer, tribulations, spiritual warfare, etc., therein lies the peace and blessings of the Lord.

I now ask you to pray with me, for the keeping power of Jesus Christ, to keep growing in Him and to share this good news about Jesus Christ with others.

Chapter 2
Mother's Death: Tradition's Effects of the Blessed Virgin Mary

The events that will take place are facts, in regard to trying to live up to the faith in which I was brought up, which is the Roman Catholic Faith. It doesn't seem important at this time to go into the trials, heartache, tribulations, etc., in one's life, because we all have experienced these. The important message I want to convey is life, according to our faith. In my heart, I have always wanted to have a close walk with our Lord and Savior, Jesus Christ. The church was, and is, a great part of my life. It was the most important aspect of my life. Along with Jesus, I had a great devotion to the Blessed Virgin Mary. I didn't realize it, but I found myself praying very much to her. However, having grown in faith and knowledge, I realize that Jesus is Lord, and it is to Him that I must pray. We must get things into perspective. No one is to take priority over Jesus. In the past, too much emphasis was put on Mary and the Saints. So many of our young children, having been schooled in the Catholic system, say that they heard more about Mary and the Saints than they did about Jesus. I found that so many people, who were having problems, were praying to the Saints and to Mary. However, after getting into the word of God, the Bible, and studying the word myself, I soon realized fully that Jesus Christ is Lord. "Thou shall have no other gods before me." Everything had to get into the right positioning. All glory and honor is His! We can, and are, ministered to by His Holy Spirit. Nowhere in Scripture can we find that we are to pray to the Saints. This must be stopped, and the focus should be where it rightfully belongs, and that is to our Lord and Savior, Jesus Christ.

Mary was a mere human being and is now dead, along with

all of the saints. And contacting the dead leads into necromancy, which is strictly forbidden by God. Jesus said, "Ask anything in my name and it shall be given unto you." (John 14: 12,14). No other name! This is extremely important, for it is how so many so-called cults that come into being enlist their faith in other people, rather than the one true Savior, Jesus Christ. Unity will only come through Jesus, not denominations or religions. If this position of men is not in accord with God's plan, it is extremely difficult for the woman. The following position must take place, also with mankind: first Jesus, then man in submission to his Lord and Savior, the only one, His majesty, Lord Jesus Christ, and then woman in submission to her man. So it is written! It is not a case of who is better, for God is no respecter of persons, but we do have a role and position.

Although I hold Mary in high esteem, Jesus is Lord. Never to worship her, but I will always have great devotion to her. She will always hold a special place in my heart, and all generations shall call her blessed. Mary said, "My soul doth magnify the Lord, and my spirit hath rejoiced in of my Savior." For he hath regarded the low estate of his handmaiden: for behold, from henceforth, "all generations shall call me blessed." (Luke 1:46-48). A woman chosen by our Lord to be the one to bring our Savior into the world is the most wonderful role to fulfill. In thanksgiving, we are most devoted to her. Being a woman, wife and mother, it brought me into a closer relationship with her. All of the special days devoted to her, I looked forward to in honoring her. Remember, not worshipping her, that alone belongs to Jesus. There is a difference. One must be very careful here.

I strove diligently to adhere to all that the church professed, but in these days with all the enemies out to crucify Jesus once again, all of my efforts and energy must be put in this direction. Jesus Christ is Lord and Savior and He died for our sins!

Even in the past, Novena days were always a joy to attend. One of the outstanding events was to attend the first Saturday of each month honoring the Virgin Mary. Those will always remain a great traditional part of my life. All of this, at that time, was in order. I realize at this point and present time that the Holy Spirit is leading His people in a new way. He is now leading us into the devotion much greater, the devotion to the Sacred Heart of Jesus. Each in unity of the promises to each person that would attend these masses or worship services. Devotions to the Sacred Heart of Jesus should put aside lesser considerations and stick to the basic Christian message, which is Jesus Christ is Lord! Thou shall have no other strange gods before Him. The message He gives is "love one another." The key to this devotion is the wholehearted giving of yourself to Jesus Christ, with the determination with God's grace, to live a life like Christ, out of love for him.

Even as I try to convey this message to you all, the forces enter in, causing my typewriter to make a buzzing sound. It distracts my thoughts, but I am keeping my eye and thoughts on Jesus, rebuking the evil spirit, which now in authority, it all ceases and all is quiet and peaceful. Prior to sitting down to type, a very heavy tiredness seemed to overtake me. I just know that something is making it very difficult to get this book into print! All kinds of interference!

Getting back to the basics and the story... The greatest fun we had as youngsters was walking that mile and a half to go to church. We were always in a group, laughing and playing along the way. However, when the snow blizzards would come, it took a great deal of effort to get to our destination. Even with frozen fingers, snow and ice on our eyelids, it was all worth it to be in the family of God, praising and worshipping our God. All that the church had to offer, we were a part of. The struggle to live within the church law took some real prayer, fasting and effort. "But as many as received Him, to him He gave the power to become the sons of God, even to them that believe on His name." (John 1:12). It is from God that we need the wisdom and moral strength. This was our way of life.

Always dependant on God, we lived our lives, seeing his hand leading – in temptations, trials, in joy, tears, blood and sweat. There was always the victory in relying on Him.

All of the necessary requirements in obeying church law, along with private prayers and Sunday Mass, seemed to be leading up to something that I did not quite understand. However, coming into the fullness and presence of our Lord becomes very real. Praise and Glory to Him! All glory and honor is His. Jesus Christ is Lord!

The Struggle

Our lives seemed to be at a joyful state. The only thing missing were more children. We only had one son. How complete things would be in life if there was another child. Praise the Lord, that did come later. How great our Lord is to hear and answer.

But all of a sudden the forces were at work again. My mother became ill, my father, my sister and my husband. The forces became aware of my closeness and love for our God. They were about to throw a curve to try to get me to blame God for this entire upsetting situation. Nevertheless, this brought me into a more prayerful state. Never during any kind of sorrow or trouble did I ever turn away and blame God. That was just what the devil wanted. The forces were about to take away my joy and happiness; it became very heavy.

My mother's thyroid condition became very distressful to her; my father started ailing; my sister was operated on to have her spleen removed; and my husband was hospitalized with a staph infection. The forces were placing all kinds of obstacles in front of me, influencing me to think that this is what the Lord does. Again and again, I would pray for strength and I thank God for His keeping power, for it is at these times that the evil one entices you into areas of matter not acceptable to the Lord, to seek temporary relief, but one must stay deep in prayer at these times. Fellowship is essential with believers who are true believers. Too many people take the route of destruction during these times.

I was the oldest girl in the family, so I had to assume a great deal of responsibility: taking my mother for her doctor's appointments, making a trip to Philadelphia to a hospital for some bone marrow tests that my sister had to take. I was very much concerned about my father and later about my husband's operation. How very wonderful it was to have a son to comfort and inspire me to trust in the Lord. Already the Lord is using him, which as the years go by, I actually see him coming into the fullness of his spiritual life. However, much anxiety began to build up inside myself. Those that I loved were having so many problems and these problems were in turn affecting me, causing me a great deal of anxiety.

During the evening, not being accustomed to much alcohol, the struggle of the forces began with thoughts of, "Oh, take a drink to settle you down." These thoughts would wave in. Not thinking very seriously about this, I proceeded to do so, and then went to sleep. The next day, the same thoughts would wave in time and time again. "Oh, take a drink to settle your nerves! Then another thought with forceful power came forth, making me feel very uneasy about taking that drink. The power that came forth led me to bed without the drink. I seemed to feel at peace.

That morning, early in the morning, as I looked out of my kitchen window, which overlooked a beautiful view with many tall, large trees, I began to pray. And as I prayed, I had a vision and a feeling of the presence of the Lord. I began to feel such tremendous strength, but by the end of the day with all of the ailing people, the anxiety once again began to build. Then again in the evening, those thoughts of "Oh, go take a drink" crept in, hovering and hounding me. It was most unusual because I never had a drinking problem and was never much concerned with drinking. Only once in a while, socially, I then would have some, but never in excess. I quickly got myself into prayer and went quickly to bed.

That night, I had a very impressive dream. The dream began by my seeing myself in front of the kitchen sink, holding a glass containing alcohol. A voice was telling me to drink it and another was telling me to pour it down the sink. I struggled, listening quietly with concern and with much attention, because at that moment a picture flashed. There in the tall, large trees I saw Jesus Christ hanging, crucified in the tree. My heart ached and as I quickly poured the drink down the sink, there appeared Blessed Virgin Mary in all of her glory, hovering above a burning bush. I cannot capture the beauty in the following piece of art, although I have managed to capture the picture enough to enable me share the vision. If only it were possible to bring forth the beauty and light that accompanied it all.

Later I awoke from the dream feeling a power of strength I've never known possible. I immediately went straight to that kitchen window, looked out, and lo and behold, there perched on top of the telephone pole was the most beautiful pigeon. It was pure white and sat peacefully overlooking the garden. How wonderful

I felt to have it perched that morning. I never saw it there after that particular day. Feel something?

As time passed, my sister did regain her health, so did my husband. Mom and Dad were not feeling too great. They were beginning to slow down, however they managed to enjoy some things and to get around. Later on, Mom was scheduled for a thyroid operation. She was in good spirits when she checked into the hospital; she had a beautiful room and was quite contented. A few days later, she had the operation. She came through the operation pretty well, although the doctor had some concern about her heart. All in all, everything looked good. All that day, dad, my brothers and sisters, and I came to stay with her. It was a day filled with anxiety. It was getting late, very late, that same day of the operation. The nurse came in and said, "Why don't you all go home and get some rest? Your mother will also get some rest, and then you all can come back early in the morning."

We were all so tired and everything seemed to be in hand. I waited a little while longer after the others had left, because my brother, John, was due to come to the hospital and mom seemed anxious to see him. He had been managing a Little League baseball game and was late in arriving. He finally arrived, and mom was so happy to see him. They talked a little, but she was tired, so we wanted her to get some rest and said "good night." But as I approached Mom's bedside, she said to me, "It hurts. It hurts bad."

I bent down to kiss her and tried to comfort her. She then seemed to fall asleep. We got her a private nurse to be sure that she would be taken care of and then went home. It was about 1:30 in the morning.

We were all exhausted from the full day of concern, worry, waiting, and caring for our young children. We all retired for the night, or shall I say for the remainder of the morning, thinking that we must get up early and get back to the hospital.

After retiring to bed, approximately 4 a.m. or so, I awakened and seemed to sit up quickly in bed feeling very uneasy. I got up, went downstairs, and suddenly felt a presence in the room. It didn't frighten me, however a thought form came forth – the Blessed Virgin Mary! She seemed to convey the word of knowledge by

Note: The Virgin Mary in the arch of the tall tress. Also note the crucified Jesus Christ in the tree limbs.

saying, "I'm going to take your mother." Just as simple as that, she said it so calmly. I shook my head as to clear my mind. I seemed to say to myself, "Oh, just because mom is in the hospital, you're getting these thoughts." I then dismissed the thought and went back to bed. Just as I began to fall asleep, after an hour or so, the phone rang. I answered it and it was my father telling me to come and pick him up, that we would have to go back up to the hospital because mom had taken a turn for the worse. I immediately got dressed and went to daddy. He had already informed my brothers and sisters to meet us there. My husband drove, and gosh, it was raining. I sat in the back seat of the car, thinking and just knowing that mom was gone that quickly. The whole earth is crying, I thought, since it was raining so hard. I still was not sure and did not mention the experience or my thoughts to dad. I kept rather silent. There was a certain quietness and peace, yet great concern in the car as we rode heading for the hospital.

As we entered the hospital and headed to the floor on which mom's room was located, the nurse met us and said, "I'm sorry, but she is gone."

My heart cried out silently, the tears began to flow, but I had to stay in control. For you see, I was carrying my long awaited child. I was pregnant, of which I will backtrack and tell you more about later on in the story.

We entered mom's room and there she lay still as ever, at peace now. I remembered just last evening when I kissed her. She didn't hurt anymore, I thought. I couldn't understand why she was taken at the young age of fifty-four. That, I didn't struggle with, for the greatest consolation was the experience of the Blessed Virgin Mary's presence that early morning, telling me she was taking my mother with her. I felt so very happy that she was in such company, the company of heaven. I seemed to accept mom's death in a very joyous way. I just felt she went straight to heaven. She was such a god wife and mother, always trying to have her family have a close walk with the Lord. She sure did a great deal of praying.

Later, after trying to share this experience of the Blessed Virgin Mary, there were people who made the statement that it could possibly be an angel, other than Mary. Sometimes Satan also comes as an angel of light, portraying saints or Mary. Then there were some that believed that it was the Blessed Virgin Mary. Maybe, too, it was all in my imagination and this was all a coincidence. The struggle was taking place again; there were forces at work to confuse me, to take away the peace that I felt about my mother's death.

However, something in my spirit told me that it was Mary. I still had arguments that she is an ordinary person, and that she, too, is dead and unable to communicate with the living, etc. The strange part was that I was not trying to communicate with her, and therefore was not guilty of necromancy. This was different. She revealed herself in spirit to me. This was not in my mind at all. I finally rested in the answer that I felt in my spirit that it was her. Other forces didn't believe in the assumption because they talked about her body being buried in some tomb, and the question came forth: why then is there a tomb in Gethsemene where her body is? The different talks also state that there is no certainty of what happened to Mary. Some tale states that she was put in the tomb and then they later found it empty, etc., etc.

Now after backtracking to the moment of my going to a doctor, feeling these strange experiences prior to the other few that I have mentioned, I was always dreaming of our Lord Jesus, but also struggling with other uncomfortable forces.

As I recall one day, a terrible rainstorm began. A black cloud seemed to pass near my house, above the living room window. As it passed, I felt every nerve in my body pounding. I began to tremble. There was a thought transference that something was going to happen to my son at school. He was attending St. Ann's Monastery. I quickly went to the phone to call my husband, who was working in the vicinity of the school. I told him to go and pick up John Jr., then told him exactly how I felt. The strange part was that he, too, was thinking about him that minute and had great concern for him. He did go pick him up, and to this day we don't know what, if anything, would have happened to him if we had not followed that special leading. Something strong in my spirit tells me there was more to all of this than meets the eye. Some greater force entered in to overshadow that black cloud. Praise the Lord! I well recall the effect that hovering cloud had on me; every nerve was jumping in my body. I also remember anointing myself with oil and holy water at that time. Everything seemed to subside when I did that. If only I had the knowledge then, as I have today, by using the name of Jesus, pleading his blood and speaking in tongues. Then it could have been easier than the old methods of struggling with the forces of evil. In those old days, it sure was a long battle, playing around with all of the symbols. Jesus has the victory! In His name there is salvation!

We all seemed to settle down and enjoy the evening. We then went to bed and soon began to have a very restful time when suddenly, half sleepy-eyed, I saw at my bedside the Blessed Virgin Mary in a very protective state hovering over me. In the doorway, trying to make entrance, was a tall, black figure with a high hat. I could not see his face, thank God, because everything was blackish. I somehow realized it was the devil. I immediately began to pray. I quickly took my rosary with the crucifix and held it all night long. I suddenly realized that there was a spiritual battle taking place. I somehow felt secure in having the vision of the Blessed

PROTECTED BY
BLESSED VIRGIN
MARY
VISION
IN BED SLeepiNG
AWAKENED TO SEE
IN TH DOORWAY TRYING
TO ENTER
THE
DEVIL
COULD
NOT
ENTER
-IN

Marie C. Pepsin

Virgin Mary not allowing the devil to enter. I only wish at that moment that I had as much knowledge as I now have today of using the name of Jesus Christ, pleading the blood of Jesus and then speaking in tongues. That sure would have made the devil flee.

The next day, I immediately set up an appointment thinking, maybe, I should have a checkup because, maybe, just maybe, something was going wrong with my mind. Yet deep within, I just knew this was just a spiritual encounter and there was nothing wrong with my mind. However, I still wanted to check things out with the doctor.

As I sat in the doctor's office, I began to feel as if I were gong to have a baby, to give birth. I had a terrible back pain, no stomach pain, but felt as though I was going to give birth. I told the doctor exactly how I felt and told him that something must be going wrong with me since I was having these experiences. He assured me that he knew me and that nothing was wrong with me. It was probably that I had built up some concern over my husband's illness, but that I was all right. However, I insisted on seeing a psychiatrist, of which entailed two visits, and sure enough nothing proved to be wrong outside of my having some anxiety built up over all my loved ones being ill, the death of my mother, etc.

That was now all in the past; everyone seemed to be getting along, praise God! A special note to take notice of, was that one year later, I gave birth to a daughter. Glory to God! My long awaited child. Was this the word of knowledge, once again, of my feelings that I was gong to give birth?

The forces, however, seemed to still be around. Not realizing what was happening, not being educated in that area, I was at a loss as to what was happening. Praise God for He teaches and guides. As I look back, His hand has always been on me. I thank Him and give Him all of the glory.

These experiences continued, with dreams, too, that seemed so real. I recall this one dream in particular in which I could hear voices of people saying, "Come on. We are going to see Jesus!" There was so much excitement going on. As I looked forward, I could see so many people gone before me, rushing up a hillside. In the dream, I seemed to go toward a little hill that was to give me a preview of the event that was happening. As I climbed that hill, I seemed to stumble and fall three times, but I got up each time and kept on going. As I got to the top, I saw the most beautiful light and Jesus Christ was there with His arms outstretched to those who were coming to Him. It was the most beautiful sight. He just stood there in His magnificent white, simple robe, with the most loving emanations coming forth from Him. I have attempted to capture some of the scene that was taking place before me. But, you must realize that I could not possibly capture it in all of its glorious beauty.

Chapter 3
There Is a Satan!

The Holy Spirit began teaching me so many things about people and life. There was an alcoholic who lived in the neighborhood, who at times would roam among the houses asking people for a drink or some money to go down to the store to buy his own. Several times, my husband would talk to him, but the man never heard a word he said. All he thought of was that drink. He would plead and beg, and after a while we sometimes gave him some money and sometimes not. Hopefully, at times, we tried to reach him in other ways. If only at that time we had the knowledge to pray with him, in the name of Jesus, pleading the blood of Jesus and speaking in tongues, it could have helped him so much in taking authority over the demons that were hovering over him. Talking to him about Christ would have been the greatest gift to give him. He seemed to get himself together at times, but every so often would go on these binges and go from house to house, pleading for a drink. He looked terrible! He smelled awful, and his pants were all wet and dirty from the duty. We all had great concern for him. His mother was senile, and she, too, would wander about the neighborhood and looked terribly lost. The understanding neighbors would gently lead her back home, but then, too, there was not much one could have done for her. If only we had recognized the Holy Spirit power and used it with the great expectation that we now have today, maybe things could have been different in that neighborhood.

One day, I was in our family den when all of a sudden God showed me for a split second what an alcoholic goes through. It all passed so quickly, and it is so hard to explain. Something terrible seemed to sweep over my body. Nausea built up beyond belief, and a power-force was knocking my body down and sending it into a state of oblivion. All alcoholics should realize that there are demonic forces that sweep over them, causing their misery. When this begins to happen – before taking a drink – you need to get to prayer fast. Immediately get someone to pray with you. Pray in the name of Jesus Christ, plead the blood of Christ and hopefully pray for the gift of tongues. This will clear the air around you and ward off that evil very quickly. "Put on the whole armour of God, that ye may be able to stand against the wiles of the devil. For we wrestle not against flesh and blood, but against principalities, against powers, the rules of the darkness of this world, against spiritual wickedness in high places." (Eph. 6:11-12). Don't let Satan get an advantage over you, be not ignorant of his devices.

When this terrible force sweeps over the alcoholic, I was told that sometimes a complete loss of time occurs, sometimes as much as three days. I actually was shown all of this while without the use of alcohol. Oh, my Lord, even in His demonstration, as though a protective hand was protecting me, for the powerful force threw my body down, He made sure there was a soft sofa to fall into. I wondered at that time if the alcoholic fell on hard ground. Pray for the alcoholic, please! It is a terrible state to be in.

Ironic as it may seem, the teaching did not stop there. The following Sunday, at Holy Mass during the priest's homily, he spoke of the situation where people, who were leading saintly lives and walking close to the Lord, sometimes went through many crises states with the forces of evil. He mentioned, in particular, the incident of one saint whom the forces of evil pushed and knocked down the stairway. The evil one gets into a rage when he sees a person having a close walk with the Lord. When I sat and listened to the priest, I sat quietly and fully understood what happened to me. It was just what I needed, for I probably would have thought that, again, I was losing my mind with all that was taking place. What a consolation it was to hear that priest talk about that subject that particular morning. You see, God also confirms things through other believers, to keep things in perspective. Praise the Lord! How wonderful it was to begin to understand the world of the spiritual realm.

SATAN RELEASED
FROM THE PIT OF HELL
GONE OUT INTO THE WORLD
26
SKETCH
DREAM VISION

The Struggle

During these intense moments of the struggle going on, knowing the people were experiencing confusion, I saw this vision in a dream. It was Satan being unleashed from a pit. It was so simple, I saw just his huge figure, all black, come out of a black pit and go into the world.

Much began happening in society, etc. Things got quite heavy, especially among the children and our youth. Unless our children pray and get under the blood of Jesus Christ, there will be turmoil and torment in their lives. They will have no peace of mind. Satan is alive! Youth pray together, I implore you! Walk close to our Lord and live according to His word to clear the hovering that takes place around you all. Jesus loves you; get under his power! The spiritual warfare is going on and is going to get heavier. The antichrist is on the scene and Christians had better band together regardless of dogmas or doctrines. They must stay together and stop tearing up the body of Christ.

Satan is gaining entrance into many lives that are being led to self-destruction. Involvement in many areas of the occult is affecting families. If one member of a family is involved in any of these areas, it can be affecting other members in that particular family. Read Isaiah 47: 9, 13-14: "These things shall come to thee... in a moment in one day, the loss of children and widowhood for the multitude of thy sorceries, and for the great abundance of thine enchantments. Thou art wearied in the multitude of thy counsels. Let now the astrologers stand up and save thee from these things that shall come upon thee. Behold, they shall be as stubble; the fire shall burn them; they shall not deliver themselves from the power of the flame." There are numerous scriptural writings in regard to the occult, pay heed do not be involved in any of the so-called "up with the times." Delving into these areas, like crystal ball, reincarnation, white and black magic, e.s.p., witchcraft, necromancy, seances, fortune telling, tarot cards, palmistry, numerology, etc., in some instances opens the door for demon oppression or even possession and insanity. These things are an abomination in the eyes of the Lord, and those of you who do not repent and get clean from such things are doomed for the lake of fire. Revelation 21:8: "sorcerers...shall have their part in the lake of fire, which burneth with fire and brimstone: which is the second death."

Beware of some of the teaching that is going on in schools and aimed toward our children. It's dangerous!

Deuteronomy 18:10-14: "There shall not be found among you anyone...that uses divination, or an observer of times, or an enchanter, or a witch, or a charmer, or a consulter with familiar spirits (which is a medium), or a wizard or a necromancer (one who makes contact with the dead). For all that do these things are an abomination unto the Lord: and because of these abominations, the Lord thy God doth drive them out from before these. Thou shalt be upright with the Lord they God. For these nations which thou shalt possess hearkened unto observers of times (zodiac study) and unto diviners: but as thee, the Lord thy God hat not suffered so to do."

Leviticus 19:31: "Regard not them that have familiar spirits, neither seek after wizards, to be defiled by them: I am the Lord your God." Leviticus 20:6, 27: "...And the soul that turns after such as have familiar spirits, and after wizards, to go whoring after them, I will even set my face against that soul and will cut him off from among his people. A man also or woman that hath a familiar spirit, or that is a wizard, shall surely be put to death."

Destroy any ouija boards or whatever devilish instruments used to receive messages from spirits, which are devils. These are not harmless games as some of you think. "I will be a swift witness against the sorcerers...For I am the Lord, I change not." Malachi 3:5, 6.

Read 1 Chronicles 10: 13, 14 also 1 Samuel 28:1-19. Read Acts 8: 9, 20, 23.

It is very important that any dealing with the occult must be confessed and repented of. All books and gadgets must be burned and then turn to get under the blood of Jesus to be cleansed, to have a new life. In Acts 19:19,20: "And many that believed came, confessed and showed their deeds. Nay of them also which used arts, brought their books together and burned them before all men; and they counted the price of them and found it fifty thousand pieces of silver. So mightily grew the word of God and prevailed."

Read Acts 13:6-12, Acts 16:16, 18, Revelation 22:14,15 and don't be fooled about reincarnation. Read Hebrews 9:26: the demons who dwelt in people in prior centuries dwell in other demon-possessed people now. It is appointed unto men ONCE to die, but after this the judgment.

Be aware: Satan is out to render you ineffective as a testimony for Jesus Christ (Peter 5:8). He will do his best to devour you by weakening you to a point where he can attach an evil spirit to you. Always in moments such as these, we overcome Satan by the blood of the Lamb and by the word of our testimony (Rev. 12:11). Overcome Satan by telling him what the blood of Jesus Christ does for you, and that his lease on your lives is not valid and has no affect on us.

Just watch and see how if he can't get to you, and you are witnessing for the Lord, how quickly he will round about and try to ruin your witness by getting at a member of your family to try to establish that there is insanity in the family. He plants a person in your life to lead you to believe this. He will manipulate members of your family so much. Be aware of this! Don't let him drag you down through another member of your family. Sometimes, most of your time should be taken in prayer with your family to make them as strong as you are in the Lord. It takes a great deal of patience and fortitude. Be wise to Satan's ways. Don't let him oppress you by his working through these very close friends and family.

After much questioning as to what was happening in regard to these unusual experiences, I knew that these were the gifts of the Holy Spirit and that we should receive all that God has to offer. Not fully understanding the realm of these supernatural situations led my mind into great exploration. If only I had the knowledge I have today and known that I should have been led by the Holy Spirit, not the mind or conscience. The conscience, or mind, can be a playground for the devil.

I realized that my father had many times experienced the word of knowledge, however he also did not understand what was happening. Many times, these experiences caused him much anxiety. He, too, would know things that were about to take place, and he would take a drink of alcohol to calm himself down. What progress he would have made if he had a dream similar to mine, if perhaps he would have gotten into prayer, etc., as I did. It was very important to have a close walk with God at these times. He was a terrific man, good husband and father. A fantastic man in life, I loved him dearly. He was a hard-working man, always filled the hours with work. Raising five children was a full time job. No matter how busy he was, one thing he always made time for was to sit on the back porch in the evening and talk with us, his children. It was then that if we had anything to discuss, or if there was anything bothering us that needed to be talked out, it was then that it was taken care of. Many times we resolved much of the problems that arose, and sometimes did not, but the discussions were always very interesting. We always appreciated the time he gave us. I only wish he had been in closer fellowship with believers. He could have handled these experiences in a much better way. At this late date, I now realize Dad did not know how to handle this because no one taught him anything in regard to all of this. It really started to do him in. I, too, not having the knowledge in this area that I have today, wasn't much help at that time. Dad still stayed close to the church, but I don't believe he had the kind of spiritual direction that he so much needed. Consequently, things got out of hand with dad, his circulation became bad, and some senility set in, along with other complications. He had fallen and broken his hip and then broken his arm. An infection did occur after his operation on the hip. A short time later, Dad died from a staph infection.

Prior to his death, even then the experiences, for me, did not cease. I lived many miles away from Dad, my heart was always with him, and I had much love and concern for him knowing just that he was not well. The year before he was hospitalized, I took care of him and enjoyed it very much. The thing I enjoyed most was knowing he could not take care of himself the way he should. I used to wash, shave and dress him in fresh clean clothes, making him look all clean and sparkling, knowing he felt so good afterward. That always made him happy. The circulation was bad, and it was to his benefit that he had around-the-clock care, so he was hospitalized. It broke my heart to do this, but he required so much care, it was exhausting my family and me. My daughter needed some care to, and that is a story in itself. It was best for everyone involved. Dad was so good otherwise, never got into anything, but needed around-the-clock watching. I prayed a great deal for him and the people involved in taking care of him. My dear son was such a blessing, whereas he spent much time with his grandfather in caring for him. Lord, take good care of him! If I can't be with him, please find someone to love and care for him as I would! I didn't realize how short dad's time was.

One night I had fallen asleep, and again, waking up suddenly in the middle of the night, I could hazily see Jesus Christ in the doorway of my room. I couldn't see very clearly, but like a fading image as I woke up. Jesus said, "It's time for your father." I began to cry and sob saying, "Oh, please not yet. It had not been too long since my mother died." These were two of the greatest people in my life, outside of Jesus Christ.

God did grant my plea, for Dad did come to live with us for a year, prior to all that came in the end. It certainly was a comfort to remember the vision of Jesus in my doorway when he died. I felt good because I just knew Dad was with Jesus. I now could handle that, even though my loss had been great.

It really was a wonderful experience with the death of my mother and father, the presence of the Blessed Virgin Mary with my mother's death, and the vision of Jesus Christ in the event of my father's death. It never occurred to me, but then I thought and asked this question, "Does Mary come for the women and Jesus for the men to usher them to their heavenly places?" Nevertheless, I thank God for the comfort and blessing of my parents' deaths.

Shortly after Dad died, I dreamed that I heard a voice telling me to listen and to pay attention! The voice proceeded to say, "Eat figs for senility!" It was that simple. I wondered if there was any value to that dream.

The word "fig" is used 64 times in both testaments – 40 times in the Old Testament and 21 times in the New Testament. The first mention is when Adam and Eve sewed fig leaves together to make aprons for their nakedness (Genesis 3:7). Fig trees abounded in Palestine, and figs are mentioned as one of the fruits of Canaan (Num. 13:23, 20:5, Dt. 8:8, Judg. 9:10,11). Figs which were used as food the year around were said to possess medicinal properties

The following sketch is of the vision in the doorway.

(2 Ki. 20:7, 1Chr. 12:40, Isa. 38:21). In Isaiah 38:21, it is written, "For Isaiah said, 'Let them take a lump of figs and lay it for a plaster upon the boil and he shall recover.'"

The strange part of this all was that having the staph infection, there had been like broken boil-like sores on Dad's foot and other areas. It now all seems that the word of knowledge was given now to understand all of this. Why I did not receive all of this information during Dad's illness, I can't answer. However, it was only after he had died that I tried and searched for answers that they seemed to come. Still, I ask if there is any value to all of this? I question again and again if figs help in any way for bad circulation?

Chapter 4
The Missionary Priest

In conjunction with my father and his experiences, my daughter, as a very young child, began to have similar happenings. For example, she knew the names of people she had never met. For instance, I was at a resort beach and we stopped at a back porch restaurant for a snack. The waitress came by and just as she was about to say, "My name is," my daughter spoke out her name. The waitress then asked, "How did you know my name?" My daughter said, "Oh, I do that sometimes, and it sometimes frightens me as to how I do know." We all shrugged it off. Also, I remember when she was very little, I was driving my car and came to an intersection to stop for a red light. No other cars were in sight when she, sitting on the seat next to me, just looked about and said, "Father Melchyer." I couldn't understand why she said that, but after a few minutes of waiting for the light to change, there driving past me came Father Melchyer. I looked at her sitting there and was amazed at the whole incident. Coincidence? All right, I began to say to myself, "So what?" I passed it off. Much to my amazement, my daughter would say words and phrases before they were even said on a television program. I had great concern and curiosity in regard to all of this. She had so many other experiences that I shall write another book in regard to all of her early years. She was such an interesting child to me. I enjoyed every minute I was with her. Yet at times, certain people, and again I stress "certain people," had much difficulty relating to her. There was so much for them to understand about her, but what a difficult time it was to have them all understand all the added extra vibrations this child was able to pick up, all the undertones of another's personality, etc., so much more. Things the average person would never be aware of.

The Struggle

I then reached out, in talking to a missionary priest about all of these experiences, at one time in the confessional. He then invited me to come to the rectory and talk. I took my young baby with me, but you must realize the experiences of this child were not in effect as yet of what I have previously written. Having the baby with me did cause some distraction from time to time because of feeding her and changing her, etc., etc. The missionary priest began with a testing of sorts, asking me, "What do I have on my mind?" And if I could tell him, this possibly could be of great help to him. At that precise moment, I could not. I could not turn whatever this was off and on at will. It had to come in God's time, not mine. We talked a great deal about many things, and intermittently he would ask me if I knew what the word that he had in his mind. No, I did not, even at that time. Again, we proceeded to talk some more. It was getting late. The school children were coming out of school and I wanted to get home when my son came in from school. I always liked being there to greet him. I immediately got up, thanked him for his time, intending to send him a donation at a later date. He told me as I was getting ready to leave to write to him after a year. I then said, "Oh, you will forget all about me by then." He smiled, "No, I'll remember you Marie, Marie Pepsin." He said some other things, and vaguely among the other words in his conversation, he used the word "computer." His face seemed to light up so brightly, smiling, with a definite confirmation of something. I didn't realize what the situation was at the time because my mind was on the distraction of the baby, coupled with the thought of getting home to my other child. Much later one, on my way home, I soon realized the word computer was the word he had in his mind, asking me what it was in that little testing encounter.

The struggle beings, forces of doubt, words coming forth, "Oh, stop that nonsense! What a fool you have made of yourself!" etc., etc. I later sent a note of thanksgiving, along with a check for twenty-five dollars, appreciating and thankful for the time he spent with me. I did not mention any of the word "computer" or any of the details because I wanted to put this whole matter behind me and to stop making such a fool of myself.

I soon received a short note thanking me for the money and a pamphlet containing some message having to do with smiling.

As time when on, I really tried to put all this behind me. Alas, sooner or later the whole episode would come forth and I thought that I should write again to the missionary telling him that I knew the word. But with the distraction of the baby, I just couldn't have it all together that day, et., etc.... The struggle soon began. "Don't do it. It all is so silly! Don't make a fool of yourself again. Stop this nonsense!" But something greater than me led me to write to the missionary. I wrote an explanation of many things in regard to this whole experience. Well, as time went on, I received not one word of response. A year went by, still no answer. Here again, the struggle begins.

Different thoughts would wave in like "he must be on a new assignment and not at that location. After all, he is a missionary, and maybe the letter got lost in the shuffle." Then, perhaps he doesn't even remember me and what this is all about. He can be very busy and lose track of all that ask him to minister to them. All of these thoughts kept running through my mind. Also, the struggle of a disappointing moment of thought was, "Boy, when I sent him twenty-five dollars, he sure did answer fast." I then asked the question, "Is money all that he is interested in?"

All kinds of struggling thoughts came in, especially reading all about a certain priestly order recently convicted of misappropriating funds supposed to be used for the poor and other worthwhile causes. I couldn't stop thinking in the effect what certain newspaper articles mentioned, that when people sent a little more money in the envelopes, they would be taken care of with a note or whatever, and the others were thrown into the wastebasket. It made me wonder about our so-called spiritual directors that came to preach and used just a lot of words, empty words!

Still, I must not judge and not think that way, but it was awfully hard not to. However, I must give him the benefit of the doubt and write him how important it was for me to hear from him. I then wrote another short note. Still, after a long time, no reply. I struggled to leave the whole situation alone. Something made me call to see if he was still with his order, for during these times of crisis in faith, so many have left the priesthood. I made a long-distance call inquiring as to whether he was still with the order. I was told that yes, he was. I did not go into any detail of what the situation was all about with the person who answered the phone; I simply called to se if he was still there. To this day, everything is still not settled. I do not understand all of this. The struggle of maybe, just maybe, he chalked me up as being a loony??? Was he happy to get ride of me??? I still say I do not understand, but I surely have done my part in whatever is taking place. To me, it is finished as far as the missionary priest is concerned.

I must be honest and say I feel very disappointed in that missionary priest. I would have felt much better and had more respect for him if he told me that he thought, maybe, I had a mental problem and needed to go to a doctor, or whatever, instead of leaving a person without a word. It is all so confusing.

The struggle for respect goes on, in view of the talk and reports of this certain order of priests only taking the letters that contained money. So many in the various orders are caught up in the money situation and are feeling very insecure. Oh, men of little faith! The test is on. Why don't you go about your Father's business as He intended? Your people are watching and waiting, so desirous of tithing, but yet have been so disillusioned as to where God's work is truly being done. So much money is being used in the wrong directions, so much mismanagement. Those who love the Lord are anxious to tithe, but have not the heart to tithe to the church that allows moral issues, such as alcohol, gambling, etc, in the place where Christ should be preached, and much spiritual food gotten. One man's tithe, I stress, only one man's tithe would take care of all the gambling and alcohol affairs that are sponsored, without breaking down the moral issues in the church. So many others would begin to tithe, so why are they spiritually blind? You who are in authority, can't you all see what is happening? Don't you care? Little by little you are getting away from God's holy word, the bible. Do not be deceived! Sort out the men of God from those who are not just passing time, feeding on the emotions of people. The struggle goes on for those who are truly concerned to bring the people out of the spiritual darkness and to be shown through God's word.

Chapter 5
Love and Concern Mystery Girl

The experiences continue with love and concern for so many people. The one that seems to be a burden upon my heart is mystery girl still battling for her life. She has been in a bad coma for so long. Her amazing inner strength has baffled many people. There is such hope that one day she will open her eyes. With all this concern, during the course of time one night while in bed sleeping, I once again had a dream about a person in a coma. It was a simple dream, but I seemed to be holding an Easter lily or a Calla lily. Here again is the struggle. Everything was a little hazy, but I seemed to weed out the Calla lily to pick out the Easter lily. Weed out loniflorum eximium and use L. Harrisii (the common Easter lily). As I moved from side to side under the person's nose, the lily, I mean the scent or whatever, seemed to permeate the room. That person began to open her eyes and come out of the coma.

As I began to awaken, I realized that there was a great lesson to be learned here. I thought nothing of the whole episode, and thought that maybe it was just a dream with nothing else to develop. As time went on and still goes on, the dream still keeps popping up, so here I am writing about it. Something greater than myself leads me on. I now turn to scripture. The scripture I am now led to is Hosea 14:5-7: "I will be as the dew unto Israel: he shall be as the lily, and cast forth his roots as Lebanon. His branches shall spread and his beauty shall be as the olive tree, and his smell as Lebanon." And now the most important message, Hosea 14:7, "They that dwell under his shadow shall return; they shall revive as corn, and grow as the vine: the scent thereof shall be as the wine of Lebanon." And moving on, Hosea 14:9, "Who is wise, and he understand these things? Prudent, and shall know them?

For the ways of the Lord are right, and the just shall walk in them: but the transgressors shall fall therein."

There is much importance to this word, "scent." Pay heed men of qualification! There is value in all that has been written. God uses us all to solve these problems.

The struggle goes on. How can we minister to mystery girl? Fill her room with Easter lilies? Medicine made from the Easter lily? Then we get one person ridiculing the whole experience. Something in my spirit tells me it is Satan working through that person. He sits there smiling, smiling, ridiculing, ridiculing, and snickering. The whole room is filled with confusion. The other eight people seem to be caught up in the spirit and feel the presence of the Holy Spirit. We are now led to begin to pray. Everyone was caught up in prayer. We all prayed for the girl. The Lord was working something even at the time which we did not fully understand, but prayers sure did go up for the girl that night. I must mention that our prayer group had met some time after that dream, and while praying and praising God, the word "lily" came forth and I then began to recall my dream, along with the experience that night, and one thing led to another. I was led to scripture Hosea 14:5,6, and then Ann said, "Look at seven." That was the most important, to me, to get it all together. Again I quote from scripture, "I will be as the dew unto Israel: he shall grow as the lily, and cast forth his roots as Lebanon. His branches shall spread, and his beauty shall be as the olive tree, and his smell as Lebanon. They that dwell under his shadow shall return; they shall revive as the corn, and grow as the vine: the scent thereof shall be as the wine of Lebanon."

In reference to the Biblical number seven, it refers to and is connected to completeness, perfection, and bringing to an end. It is wise to remember that other numbers have significance also. Thus the heavens and the earth were finished, and all his work which he had made: and He rested on the seventh day from all of his work which he made (Genesis 2:1,2). And ye shall count unto you from the morrow after the Sabbath, from the day that ye brought the sheaf of the wave offering, seven Sabbaths shall be complete (Leviticus 23:15). But in the days of the voice of the seventh angel, where he shall begin to sound, the mystery of God should be finished, as he hath declared to his servants the prophets (Revelation 10:7). And the seventh angel poured out his vile into the air: and there came a great voice out of the temple of heaven, from the throne, saying, it is done (Revelation 16:17). And it came to pass after seven days, that the waters of the flood were upon the earth (Genesis 7:10).

The number eight refers biblically to new birth. In the new birth, a person becomes a new creature, through the divine nature of God. And Abraham circumcised his son Isaac being eight days old, as God commanded him (Genesis 21:4). Search scripture for more on the number eight. You will begin to see the perfect system, Bible system, of numbers that fit together to form a God plan of numbers.

Draining from all the love and concern of the issues that were brought forth to be laid upon my heart, which became a burden to me, as if the Lord wanted me to be concerned about these issues. In summary are the following key words:

CANCER: Moth, death. Butterfly, life. Poisons...picked up, but also hovering from flower to flower are living museums of natural drugs. Then, too, if you accidentally ate a monarch butterfly, you would become violently ill. Beware of these critters hovering on the foods that we eat. Just watch the tobacco being dried and see the moths hovering around. It's deadly. Once again I stress the association of the moth with cancer. The clothes moth, key word also. More to come in Chapter 6, The Cancer Dream.

ARTHRITIS: Weeping willow leaves.

BALDNESS: Honey comb, a structure of wax containing rows of hexagonal cells, formed by bees for the reception of honey and pollen and of their eggs. Any substance, as a casting of iron, etc., having cells like those of a honeycomb. The reticulum of rumnant. Having the structure or appearance of a honeycomb, honeycomb weave. To reduce to a honeycomb, pierce with many holes or cavities. A rock honeycombed with passages. To penetrate in all parts.

HONEY: Biblical, honey can sometimes mean a thick grape or fig syrup. Besides that there was wild honey and honey that was produced and counted among the fruits of the field (Deut. 32:13, Ps. 81:16, 2 Chron. 31:5). Honey was not used in sacrifice, because, like the leaven which was also prohibited, it fermented easily (Lev. 2:11). John the Baptist's food was locusts and wild honey (Matt. 3:4, Mk. 1:6), and his disciples offered the risen Christ at his request some grilled fish and a honeycomb, which he ate before their eyes, sharing the leftover with them (Lk. 24:43). Parsley also fits in somewhere in this picture????

SENILITY: Figs, rest of this is written elsewhere in this book.

COMA: Easter lily. Calla lily, the explanation is also in more detail in this book.

ALCOHOLISM: Mimosa leaves, especially the flowers.

OBESITY: Fat, infrared, the part of the invisible spectrum contiguous to the red end of the visible spectrum, comprising radiation of greater wavelength than that of red light. Denoting or pertaining to the infrared or its component rays.

Also the key Gospel is 2 Thessalonians 2:6,12: And now ye know that withholdeth that he might be revealed in his time. For the mystery of iniquity doth already work: only he who now letteth will let, until he be taken out of the way. And then shall that Wicked be revealed, whom the Lord shall consume with the spirit of his mouth, and shall destroy with the brightness of his coming. Even him, whose coming is after the working of Satan with all power and signs and lying wonders. And with all deceit of unrighteousness in them that perish; because they received not the love of the truth, that they might be saved. And for this cause God shall send them strong delusion, that they should believe a lie: That they all might be damned, who believe not the truth, but had pleasure in unrighteousness.

If there is great confusion entering in, rebuke it in the name of Jesus, plead the power of His blood, and speak in tongues to clear it all away. It is hot, too, but nevertheless all things must come to an end and a new beginning tomorrow. It is wise at this point to take a rest from your reading for this is a heavy chapter.

We are all now wondering if we really draw on the power of the Holy Spirit when sickness hits us, or do we stop and say, "God, put this on me, and I must accept this." We must now remember the other force is around and we must refuse to accept it if we are truly a child of God. Rebuke it in the name of Jesus!

God wants his children to be healthy. Always seek the leading and guidance of the Holy Spirit in any matter, yes, even sickness.

There came a time when there were so many people having sore throats who had to be confined to bed and stay home from work. My son and I talked together and wondered if they really had drawn upon the power of the Lord. Low and behold, a few days later, I began to get a sore throat. I immediately asked for the leading and guidance of the Holy Spirit. I didn't wait, but prayed as soon as I detected any slight infection and didn't accept any of it by saying, "Gee, I have a sore throat." I followed the leading and was led to drink the natural limeade frequently during the day, plus approximately four tetracycline capsules, one ever four hours. Praise the Lord for His guidance. I did not have to be confined or take any time off, for I continued with my work as usual, and I did conquer it before it got me. There is victory in the following of the Holy Spirit's guidance. However, be sure your walk with Christ is a close walk, or you may be inclined to hear the wrong voice. Be very careful in this area.

With love and concern, we must be very much in tune with the Holy Spirit, even when we are called to pray for someone. Sometimes it is wrong to pray for them to remain here with us when God is calling them back home. This, too, is a touchy area. We must seek the Lord during these times, always pray for the salvation of that person, to have them know about Jesus and to accept Him as their Lord and Savior. This is the all important, for as it is written in Holy Scripture, "No one comes to the Father, but through me." Jesus said that himself. To be under the blood of Jesus by believing that He died for our sins is the all important issue. If you do not accept this, you will then die in your sins. It is written!

We must have a close walk with the Lord, to follow his leading in any matter that we are called on to pray for. Through His help, we then can be of help to others. Prayer has power! Use it with wisdom. Be in tune with His power. Sometimes it is with prayer that we give them over to Christ to be taken into their heavenly home. It is our utmost prayer that they do not suffer, but have a happy death and a peaceful death. It is not meant for God's children to suffer and be unhappy at the time of departing from this world.

The Struggle

The joy of being home with the Lord for all eternity is certainly life in all its fullness. Surely, it is in His time, not ours, that we are received into the Heavenly glory. Until then we must be of service in this world, even if we are not of the world, especially to bring the good news to others who have not heard about Jesus. Sometimes there are other roles to fulfill, but there must always be time for God's word to be brought forth in some way that the Lord has planned for you.

It certainly is an adventure to watch how the Lord works in one's life. It is unbelievable! Resist temptations that are not in accord with God's word. Be strong in the Lord and watch how the blessings pour forth! It is great to serve the Lord. He is the greatest! Praise, honor and glory! Jesus is Lord! He loves us and is concerned about us. Allow Him into your life and let His power begin to work in you. You will flower out beyond one's imagination. Your peace will be unbelievable; your joy, your final attainment.

Chapter 6
The Cancer Dream

My brother's wife became ill, ailing, which turned out to be cancer of the uterus. Before she realized it, the cancer had spread. Evidently the doctor did not detect it early enough. I just couldn't believe such a wonderful young person, just at her prime in life, 42 years old, was going to die. The doctors had given up any hope, and to keep giving her more blood transfusions would only prolong her agony. It was decided between her doctor and husband to just let her go peacefully and let her fall asleep and go to her Lord. However, there were other forces who thought otherwise, who did decide to give her blood without the consent of her husband, which proved later to cause her great suffering.

All kinds of forces interfered. What a mess was made of everything and everybody. During this time, all kinds of forces entered in to complicate matters such as fighting, opinions, restrains on her visitors, etc. What a terrible mess! My God, I thought, why didn't people mind their own business and leave that young couple alone. Things would have worked out so much better. Everyone thought they would do better than the next. All had their own selfish vendettas and tried to fulfill their own convictions. Instead of allowing this young couple to make peace for the final end, they prevented this in so many ways. The husband was in such turmoil with three young children, plus a young wife about to die. All of the evil forces about certainly led him in the wrong direction, instead of him getting the support that he needed during this time of crisis. There was just added pressure that had been too great. If only he had resorted to much prayer instead of the direction of reaching out as he did. Perhaps there should be repentance for this; there will be no peace if many of these certain issues are not confessed to Jesus to be forgiven. With the hassle with the other forces, along with the pressures of holding down his job, along with the debt incurred during the illness, I often wonder how he managed to keep his sanity. Oh what a terrible ordeal. The people forces caused much more damage than enough.

The Bible states, "Vengeance is mine: I will repay, saith the Lord." (Romans 12:19). No one should avenge themselves, for it is written. Be not overcome with evil, but overcome evil with good. If only these people would accept this teaching, everything could have turned out much better. So many people make their own judgments! They think themselves wise with their own conceits and make such a mess of everyone's life!

What God has joined together, let no man put asunder! No man! What a terrible end, with so many to account before God in this final judgment. What a terrible struggle! Let no man judge, lest he be judged.

I seemed to watch and evaluate all that was happening, and my spirit was crying out that the only important thing now was to try to give that young man and young woman some peace and stop all this fighting.

During all the events that took place, along with the illness, I'm sure her husband can write a book. However, the woman dying of cancer, my husband, and I seemed to have a very good relationship. But every time I would go to see her, my heart would cry out silently, "I can't believe she is gong to die!" Her children were practically raised to where she would have some time to herself and now this terrible cancer. We seemed to have nice visits with her, but living away from the area prevented frequent visits, plus the fighting that would be going on around her, with the people who took her away from her husband, was always a hassle. Wanting to give her some peace, we just let her alone. She was constantly on our minds, but with the stronghold she was under, to try to do anything would only be more upsetting to her. And she had enough to contend with, so we left her alone, not discussing any of the issues.

My only regret is that I had not grown in the spiritual knowledge, that I now have, to have been able to minister to her and rebuke the evil forces around her at that time. It is only now that I possess more spiritual light.

My God, at that time I kept saying. "My God, what can I do? Everyone is fighting when we should be in prayer!"

That night, I knelt at my bedside, tears rolling down my cheeks, sobbing, and my heart aching. I then began to pray. I ended my prayer by asking, "My God, what causes this terrible cancer?" I then got into bed and fell asleep.

That same night, I remember having a dream. In that dream, someone was telling me to LISTEN, LISTEN, LISTEN. The next thing I saw was something coming toward my ear. I said, "Is it a hummingbird?" Someone said, "No." I then said, "But it resembles a small, small hummingbird!" Again, I heard someone say, "No, not a hummingbird." Right then, the next thing that happened was that I seemed to be having this lump before me. I knew this was still in association with the cancer episode. I just knew it! After seeing this lump before me, I began running after this large orange ball, but that just seemed to pass. I then seemed to be lancing the lump, NOT cutting it out, but just lancing it in the direction of the cross of Jesus Christ. As I will stress, the cutting sign on the lump was a cross. I then seemed to be smearing it with a solution that appeared to be that of egg white, or something similar. I then woke up with the feeling that I must solve this mysterious dream with the direction and leading of the Holy Spirit. I felt a very strong leading. (As I grow in the spirit, it could be semen?)

That morning, I made my family breakfast, sent my husband off to work and sent my son off to school. I then began to read the morning paper while having my cup of coffee. As I leafed through the pages, I came across an article stating that scientists are discovering that certain operations were influenced by the MOON. I immediately had a quickening in my spirit. That was THE ORANGE BALL I WAS CHASING IN MY DREAM! I knew that in the rushing, while the moon was full, that was the key. The time for that kind of operation was when the moon is full! I was sure that part of the mystery was solved. But I realized that someone more qualified could get this issue together more. Something much greater than myself just had that particular article in the paper, that particular morning, just after the dream.

The episode continues... I then decided to spend the day in

Scranton, Pennsylvania. (I used to live in the nearby area.) I felt led to go shopping. With nothing else in mind, I boarded the bus and off I went. I entered a large department store, and as if someone had led me to a book department, I seemed to go right to a particular book, just as simple as that. I opened it and felt a quickening, for in that book on a page was a hummingbird hawk moth. A voice within said, "There is what you saw in your dream! You couldn't get it together during your sleep, but that is what you saw."

The struggle begins with all kinds of forces zeroing in. Does a MOTH cause cancer? How? Questions, questions, questions... voices within, voices in thoughts... "Oh, you are so silly." "Stop this nonsense," another voice said within, "one more qualified in this field will get it all together, but you have the key." "Together you will work it out." MOTH, MOTH, MOTH, DUST, DUST, DUST... These words kept coming forth. Okay, I now have the moth, moon, which is the cause and effect. The cure has yet to come forth. I begin to ask, "Does the simple white of an egg have a bearing?" The medicine I was smearing on the lump, in my dream, it sure looked like it and felt like it. I kept mulling over this treatment. Then all of a sudden, with another quickening within my spirit, came the brilliant idea that could it be semen??? Was there a curative property in it? A cure for cancer??? The struggle takes place... Was there anything of importance to this experience combined with the dream??? Should I toss it out of my mind and forget all this silly nonsense??? The voice from outside says, "Put this all out of your mind." The voice within says, "Do something with all of this information."

I let a month go by and figured that I would try to stop all of this nonsense, but I did recall that after coming home from Scranton, I just knew something within my spirit was working. Recalling... that same day I was led to the Bible. I turned the page to Isaiah 51:7,8, "Hearken to me, you that know what is just, my people who have my law in your heart: fear ye not the reproach of men and be not afraid of their blasphemies. For the worm shall eat them up as a garment and the MOTH shall consume them as wool: but my salvation shall be forever, and my justice from generation to generation."

I felt such a quickening within my heart and spirit that I quickly closed the book in utter amazement! I stood quickly for a minute and tried to compose myself. I felt such great joy! I then opened the Bible once again and immediately knew deep within my spirit that this was part of the mystery of cancer.

The struggle of the forces came in to play again. "What a stupid experience! Leave all of this alone! People will think you are crazy! What wild thing to happen," etc., etc.

Then I decided to try this whole experience on my family, telling them all about this whole episode. They listened, but didn't quite understand it all and just seemed to shrug it off. Next I thought I would try to share it with some of my friends. It was all a little confusing to them, however, here and there, they would say that maybe there was something to it. Then they plainly went about their business. Still, no satisfaction. So I put it all to rest. I tried desperately to forget it all. Just when I thought it was all over, something would cause me to pick at this whole experience and dream combined. Something or someone kept prodding me to do something about all of this.

At a later date, I was led to a group that had many experiences, and I thought that maybe they would understand what I was trying to convey. They also listened, and just seemed to listen, without many comments. Occasionally, they would bring the moth up to tease me about it. Many times I would read something about the moth, and they would remark, "Oh, not that moth again." They would sort of make fun of me. Every time they would do that, a voice within would say, "Fear not the reproach of men and be not afraid of their blasphemies." (Isaiah...). That was always comforting to me. But the forces sometimes would weaken me and I would shelve the whole matter.

The opportunity to share this experience came in a workshop on dreams. As I look back to that experience, I do believe there was a lesson there to be learned, but just in allowing me to see what the evil forces can do in these situations. As I shared some of the dream experiences, the teacher seemed all excited and elated, but somehow I felt she missed the whole point of what I was trying to convey. I knew she was interpreting this as it came to her, and that there was an excitement of good things going to happen as a result of this experience. I had a feeling of being on cloud nine. As I mention the number nine, I associate that number with the nine gifts of the Holy Spirit. The nine gifts are: "For to one is given by the spirit the word of wisdom; to another the word of knowledge by the same spirit; to another faith by the same spirit; to another the gifts of healing by the same spirit; to anther the working of miracles; to another prophecy; to another discerning of Spirits; to another diverse kinds of tongues; to another interpretation of tongues; but all these worketh that one and the same Spirit, dividing to every man severally as he will." (Corinthians 12: 8, 11).

The number nine is also associated with the nine fruits of the Spirit, which are love, peace, longsuffering, gentleness, goodness, faith, meekness, temperance: against such there is no law (Galatians 5: 22, 23).

But getting back to the workshop on dreams. It had one caught up in excitement, uncertainty, and put one in a state of ecstasy of yet not knowing what lay ahead. I had to wait until I got home to clear my mind as to all that was going on in the workshop with the teaching.

When I got home, my bubble seemed to deflate and I came back to earth, so to speak. I had to sort out what to retain in the teaching workshop and what not to. With so much marbleized information feeding in, I knew that I needed more direction in that vane so as not to go off the bounds as to what the word of God prohibits. I must have a close walk with Jesus and His teachings. Of course I must not stray, for the world is so marbleized with error and false teaching of the antichrist, so contrary to the word of God. The realm of the antichrist is so cleverly disguising the lies and trying to polish up their selfish needs, or rather I should say desires. But these issues are dealing with one's eternal destiny and better to face the truth. This is very serious business; sin is sin, no matter how you try to disguise it.

So, once again, I let the cancer dream rest. However, months later, the dream was all of a sudden back again, prodding me on again and again. I was determined to do something constructive. I decided to call a well known hospital. I then asked to talk to someone in cancer research. I was connected with a lady. I then related the moth dream to her and the association of cancer. She listened and told me she would check to see if there had been any research on the moth, then let me know if there were any cancer properties, etc. She told me later that there had been studies, but they had no bearing. I hung up after thanking her, and a voice within me said, "But they didn't research THE HUMMINGBIRD HAWK MOTH! All moths do not cause cancer, only certain ones." As all mosquitoes do not cause malaria, only certain ones. The struggle begins, "Oh, stop this foolish nonsense! What a fool you are making of yourself. Stop this or people will think you are crazy." So again, I let it rest.

Nevertheless, I felt somewhat relieved, for if I had received the word of knowledge from the Lord, I certainly was sharing the message and not having the sin of omission – not doing anything about it. For I did so, it was out of my hands now. The only leading thus far was to also write this all in this book.

To whom it may concern: I certainly now feel that my mission is over in this respect and the next servant of our Lord Jesus Christ will carry on. Praise God! Glory to the Father, all glory and honor is His! Peace to men on earth because He lives, ministering to His people.

As I close with the dream of remembering that the whole episode revolved around the voice telling me to listen, and what I vaguely saw coming toward my ear, I am now led to Job 4:12,13. It is written, and there is depth here so read carefully, "Now a thing was secretly brought to me, and mine ear received a little thereof. In thoughts from the visions of the night, when deep sleep falleth in men." Praise God! Feeling anything? Oh, glory to God!

This following page shows a sketch of the cancer dream.

Meditating on the word, "The worm shall eat them up as a garment, and the moth shall consume them as wool." (Isaiah 51:7,8). Cancer???

Isaiah 66:24, "...and they shall go forth and look upon the carcasses of the men that have transgressed against me: for their worm shall not die, neither shall their fire be quenched; and they shall be an abhorring unto all flesh."

Mark 9:44, "Where their worm dieth not and the fire is not quenched."

Job 7:5, "My flesh is clothed with worms and clods of dust;

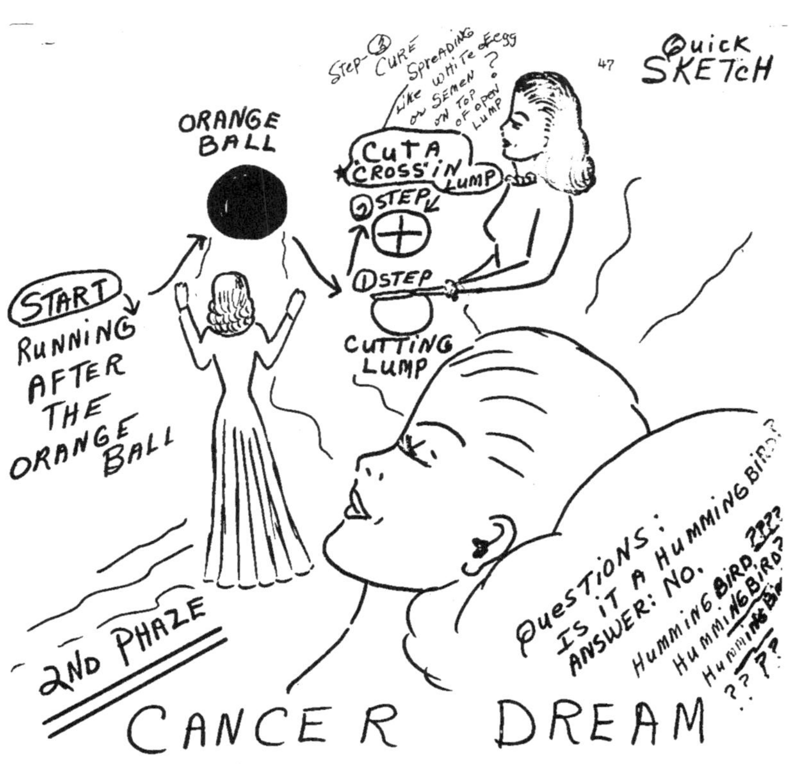

All in ONE NIGHT
PHAZE 1 AND PHAZE 2

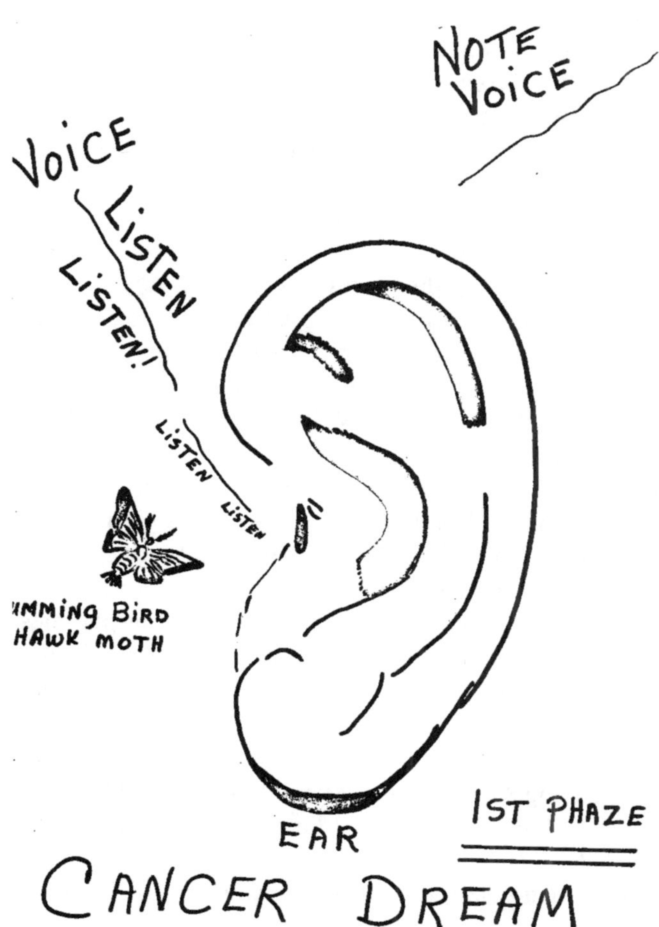
NOTE
VOICE
VOICE
LISTEN
LISTEN!
LISTEN
LISTEN
MMING BIRD
HAWK MOTH
EAR
1ST PHAZE
CANCER DREAM

my skin is broken and loathsome. Job 19:25, "And though after my skin worms destroy my body, yet in my flesh I shall see God." Job: 21,26, "They shall lie down in the dust, and the worms shall cover them!" Job 24:20, "The womb shall forget him; the worm shall feed sweetly on him; he shall be no more remembered; and wickedness shall be broken as a tree."

Continuing on in meditation on the moth...shall consume them as wool. Job 4:19,21: "How much less in them that dwell in houses of clay, whose foundation is in the dust, which are crushed before the moth? They are destroyed from morning to evening; they perish forever without any regarding it. Doth not their excellency which is in them go away?" They die even without wisdom.

Job 13:28, "And he, as a rotten thing, consumeth, as a garment that is moth eaten. How much less in them that dwell in houses of clay, whose foundations is in the dust..." Does anyone reading this understand??? LARVAE...WORMS...KEY WORDS... clothes, moth eaten... another key word.

Isaiah 50:9, "Behold, the lord God will help me; who is he that shall condemn me? Lo, they shall wax old as a garment; the moth shall eat them up." Isaiah 51:7,8, "Hearken to me, you that know what is just, my people who have my law in your heart: fear ye not the reproach of men and be not afraid of their blasphemies. For the worm shall eat them up as a garment and the moth shall consume them as wool; but my salvation shall be forever, my justice from generation to generation." This scripture was constantly on my mind, always coming forth to prod me on as if the Lord kept saying, "Marie, there is something to all of this! Get it in the hands of the right person." I kept searching. Who is the right person???

As I questioned who the right person was, one night after I had fallen asleep, I had a dream. I was going somewhere on a bus trip, and while I was sitting with someone, I began to share the cancer dream and the experience. I didn't realize that a priest was listening to our conversation. I can't remember or recall who he was or what he looked like, but he got quite involved and believed there, too, was something to this cancer dream and was going to help me. I am now waiting patiently, not planning any bust trip at this moment, however some time in God's time this bus trip will come about and this priest, whoever he is, will be on that bus, and this dream will all become a reality. As of this moment, it will be a waiting period, but I can't wait until I see God unfolding His plan in all of this. He is my great teacher and Lord. Perhaps by the time I finish this book, I will have more to report on this matter.

Getting back to some more scripture, Hosea 6:12-15: "Therefore will I be unto Ephraim as a moth, and to the house of Judah as rottenness. When Ephraim saw his sickness, and Judah saw his wound, then went Ephraim to Assyria and sent to King Jareb; yet could he not heal you, nor cure you of your wound. For I will be unto Ephraim as a lion, and as a young lion to the house of Judah; I even I, will tear and go away; I will take away, and none shall rescue him. I will go and return to my place, till they acknowledge their offense, and seek my face; in their affliction they will seek me early."

As I proceed to write, the forces begin to try and look and block my writing. I remember reading a book a few years ago that would shed some light on the cancer dream. For some unknown reason at that time, I jotted down the title of the book and the author. This book now comes to my mind, and I need to reread it. So, I called the same library from which I got it in the first place. It happened that they no longer had it in stock. For some unknown reason, they had gotten rid of some of their old books. Immediately I knew Satan had a hand in this, trying to block me from getting that certain book. I didn't leave it at that, so I asked the girl at the library to check and see if any other library would have it. She checked, and sure enough, there it was. It was at Pratt Library in Baltimore. I then asked her to really try to get it for me. She said she would, but it has been several weeks, and after several months and repeated phone calls to the library to check its whereabouts, the girl told me she would put a tracer on it. Still weeks have passed and still no word. Satan surely is blocking that book from getting into my hands. I may have to travel into Baltimore and try to get the book myself. Incidentally, the title of the book, I must say at this point, is the mystery book. Here again, I like this book and the way it is being written, being led by the Holy Spirit that even you at this time are included in this book to seek and find the whereabouts of this book! Someone out there must know where it is! Nevertheless, we will find just the key word, worm. "The worm shall eat them up as a garment, and the moth shall consume them as wool." It is not written in his book that way, but he does mention the worm. Isaiah does the rest in Holy Scripture.

There are so many forces blocking me from writing this book. So many doors are opening, enticing me to discontinue writing. Lately, after a long break, the Lord is weighing upon my heart the importance of completing this book and to not be discouraged but be determined to finish it. And He has installed in me that determination. Nothing is that important to stand in my way. Praise the Lord!

Unusual Satanic attacks are taking place. He is actually trying to attack my body, anything to distract me or take up my time with many blocks. To some this may be mere coincidence, but you who know the Lord know what I mean.

The unusual accumulation of hardened wax in my ears, along with the continual uses of hair spray, causes a loss of hearing in a sense of clogged ear wax. I have never before tried to alleviate the use of oil, recommended by my physician, with the application of flushing out the ear etc. I have always, as a result of this, had to go to a doctor's office to have it taken care of. However, living a life in the spirit, I am led in prayer to ask God, in the name of Jesus, by the power of His blood, and speaking in tongues, (praying in the spirit) by His Holy Spirit, to minister to my ear problem. Praise the Lord, His leading resulted in my doing my part, using the oil, flushing out the ear wax, which when I did it alone before, never worked. But with the aid of the Holy Spirit...Praise the Lord, it worked. Oh, I called it done! I could hear and I didn't have to make that doctor's visit as I had always done in the past in spite of all that I tried to do myself. Glory! God took over where Satan tried to attack.

This was also a great lesson learned on the difficulty of deaf people, of which I received great insight into their problems. But, if they would only accept Jesus into their lives and pray that they would receive Jesus Christ into their hearts, it would be unbelievable what He can do. Yes, I say unbelievable. There are blessings to receive when living by the word of God and accepting Him as Lord and Savior. For as many as received Him, to them

He gave the power to become children of God.

Every so often I would take a break from writing and the usual everyday work, but always had the awareness of God working in my life. I could see His hand in my life so much. What peace I began to have. Trusting Him was getting so easy; it was just wonderful, just beautiful. However, Satan was still plugging away. I wondered when he would get tired of trying and leave, but he never will stop trying to get your soul, until death. It is so important to stay close to Jesus, live by His word, have true Christian fellowship and pray always to clear the air.

Driving down to North Carolina and South Carolina, it was a beautiful trip. The scenery was so lovely and breathtaking. We had some time to meditate on the way, and constantly the word "moth" was on my mind, and then the butterfly...symbolic of life. Somewhere, some time, I must get this all together! Once again, to have all of this information flower out, so yes, that beautiful butterfly can rest on the flower. Oh Lord, I now pray! Make them whole! By the power of your Holy Spirit!

We decided to make a trip to the Carolinas in one day. It would be a long trip, but it was the 4th of July weekend, and there were no accommodations anywhere. The highways were so busy and we were getting so tired. Lo and behold, as we came to some strange territory, there was a great storm brewing. It became very dark, with dark clouds forming that seemed to hover above. It all seemed so weird. They became very threatening; visibility was getting worse as time went on. We were all so tired and there was no place to find rest.

I then seemed to meditate on the Virgin Mary, when there was no place for her to rest when she was with child. My memories, too, went back to the time when I first came to Westminster, Maryland, to visit. I, too, was with child, and when we tried to get a room in the only motel in town, there were no rooms. The manager, seeing I was with child and very tired, told us we could take their private bedroom in the back to rest. We thanked him and felt great appreciation and rested up.

Slowly my thoughts got back to the storm and driving. If only we could get to Myrtle Beach, then we would surely find something! It began to rain, which made the driving worse. I looked at my husband and saw how tired he was. The windshield wipers going back and forth seemed to make him twice as sleepy. Then I thought that I must pray for the rain to stop, at least until we got to our destination. Once again, I began to pray in the name of Jesus Christ, by the power of His blood, spoke in tongues, and praised the Lord, it worked! It stopped raining, but at the same time a dark cloud was overshadowing, and my husband began to snicker and say, "Yeah, yeah, it was just that way. It stopped, but it wasn't because of your prayer."

You see, it sometimes bothered my husband to hear me pray with such serenity and certainty, with great expectation. As he said that , a few minutes later and a short distance down the road, we ran into more rain. At once, I began to pray in the same manner as I had before. Again, it stopped. Would my husband give credit to the prayer? No way. He was still ridiculing the whole thing. I could feel myself getting angry, for I could feel the two forces battling each other again, that I must pray for him also. That seemed to clear the air around him, and lo and behold, the rain stopped completely.

I began to wonder how often the individual throws blocks, blocking the power of prayer for their lack of faith in the matter. With perseverance in prayer, there will always be the power. Jesus Christ is still on the throne. He saw our need, tired and without a place to stay, and took away the rain so we could drive in peace and be refreshed by His presence. Praise the Lord!

We can be overcomers if we have faith in Jesus Christ. He will take care of us. Believe it, stand firm on His promise. Don't let anyone put doubt there. It does work. Satan will immediately wave in, trying to plant doubt, etc., but persevere in complicated matters and he will flee. But be on guard and spiritually alert, for he will return and keep trying to smash your faith until you die. Therefore it is very, very important to stay in prayerful fellowship. Satan hates that kind of togetherness and will flee from it. He will try to break up prayer centers. He will do his utmost to have everyone fearful and flee at the least possible difficulty. Every prayer group that has started, he tries to gain entrance and have it split up. Be spiritually alert, recognize when he uses someone to destroy that fellowship. Even the elect will be deceived. Put on the whole armor of God. Satan will try to attack, but under the lordship and the blood of Jesus Christ, you will be protected.

So as I proceed to write this book, it seems that he tries to take up my time in many frivolous ways. He just doesn't want this book to be published or even written! Today as I planned to continue writing and do laundry, the water flooded all over the laundry room floor. I must confess at this point I can say it probably was my own ignorance, because it is a terribly cold day outside and the pipes and hoses could be frozen. I, at this point, am not taking the time to investigate the matter, because I must get down to my writing for my schedule is a busy one. But I can't help to question, is Satan again at work trying to hinder me?

Satan staged another attack without warning. I was trying to put a vacuum cleaner plug into an extension socket, and all of a sudden the entire end blew up in flames in my hand, melting the end of the cord and burning in my hand! The palm of my hand was black as coal, and a large blister began to form. And then a voice was saying, "Now you won't be able to type your book!" All at once my thoughts were turned to Jesus, and I was asking Him to help take over this burden. Immediately I was led to the sink to run water on the hand and to keep rubbing while the water kept running over my hand. "Rub, rub," a little inner voice kept saying. "Rub, rub and take soap along with the water and keep rubbing." Very soon all of the burned black was washed off. At first it seemed that I wanted to stop rubbing my hand, but the Lord commanded me to keep rubbing. And in persevering, immediately all of the blackness and slight pain left. I must stress, only a slight pain was felt in spite of the burn that I was meant to have by Satan. God once again protected me. Praise God and glory to Him! The only thing that did remain was a blister the formed on the thumb, and immediately after pricking it, the hand looked as if nothing had happened. It took an immediate response from the Lord. And since I followed His instructions, immediately the hand was healed. There was just that one interference of a voice telling me to stop scrubbing, but I recognized the counterfeit voice. That made the difference. The hand looked terrible from the beginning, and now it looked as though nothing happened. Call on the name of Jesus, and by the power of His blood, speak in tongues, pray in spirit that heavenly language, live according to His world and believe it works!

At this point, I can hear skeptics saying, "Oh, that was just a mere happening. Why are you saying it was a Satanic attack?" Beloved, it is different when a demonic spirit is trying to influence you. It is inner knowing, and it is hard to put into words. Living a life in the spirit lets you know these things. I do believe the Lord will give us further knowledge in the near future to distinguish and to explain, in mere words, this inner knowing of what this is all about. Having the Baptism of the Holy Spirit and living according to His word, the Bible, seem to be prerequisites. Also needed are to live a life in the spirit, a life led by the spirit, the Holy Spirit, and no other, having a close walk with our Lord Jesus Christ, becoming one with Jesus Christ. That beautiful union is beyond the imagination. He is just waiting, with His arms outstretched, to receive you. I implore you, whatever state you are in, keep your mind and heart on Jesus, and with His power, He will draw you onto Him.

The following page has a sketch of my dream in which I saw Jesus Christ drawing me unto Him, in which I became one with Him. Praise God!

Our people will not be in a battle of guns and war, but in a spiritual battle, especially the dedicated men of God. In the name of Jesus Christ, they will suffer much persecution; however, they will be strong in the Lord and on their way to glory. Physical exhaustion will be their worst enemy because the evil one transfers this to the individual working for Christ. In some instances, Satan inflicts a deep sleep upon you, to slow you down in the progress of work and your enthusiastic response. The day fast approaches for one to lay down his life for the Lord. Many people have already lost their love of this earthly life, getting ready for Jesus to come and not having to look back for anything on this earthly plane. The revival of God's people must advance. Time is getting shorter and shorter. People will be confronted to make their long delayed choice of whether to accept Jesus Christ as their personal Savior or not. They have heard, dabbled around, and still have not made the commitment. Time is getting short...you must decide to step out on faith to receive Jesus Christ. The decision is yours and

QUICK SKETCH
THE DREAM
BECAME ONE WITH JESUS CHRIST

nobody else's! Once again, not my words, but those of our Savior, "No one comes to the Father, but through me." Jesus, himself, spoke these words.

In communion with my Lord, meditating on the Last Supper (oil painting), my eyes shifted to the Lord's face. I was told to look for the pure white circle on the center of the forehead. I would see a larger white circle and a smaller one underneath. This would indicate that the person was of Jesus Christ, for discerning spirits. I would see this with the eyes of the spirit.

The evil one would have the number 666. Instead of the pure white circle, a little above the center of the eyes.

In close association with those who do not accept Jesus Christ as Lord, a heavy disturbance takes hold, exhausting one to a loss of enjoying this life. It takes all of one's energy to shake the oppression that hovers about. It requires a great deal of movement to get rid of this, movement to a place of prayer, to pray unceasingly for at least an hour. The darkness soon disappears and you move on to your brothers and sisters in Christ for peace and nourishment in preparation to, once again, go out into the world and win souls for Jesus Christ.

There are so many out in the world professing Jesus Christ and making such a mockery of His teaching. My heart cries out, "People, he didn't mean it that way!" People are ridiculing each other, acting superior this and superior that. Christians, themselves, are tearing up the body of Christ. Christians unite! The counterfeit is getting his army together!

Children of God, our Lord Jesus Christ is no respecter of persons. He loves us all regardless of color, society status, etc. Some have not as yet come into the fold. They have strayed, but leave them alone for they'll come home. I am so anxious thinking how can they be so blind? The evil one sure has them bound! We must pray for them!

So many have reached out after their own lusts and have found nothing. They search in every direction, but never once ask for His will for their lives, through which there is complete peace and contentment. The evil one has them so bound, and they don't even realize it. Unhappiness and vertigo overtakes them. They rush around to keep from getting this communication with their God, our Lord Jesus Christ. If only they would realize the peace, love, joy and contentment He brings. Why can't they experience this? Because they love self, think about self, and that's the core of the whole situation. How foolish! He knows you better than you know yourself, and he knows what is best for you. Allow him to enter your lives; my heart yearns for you to allow Him in. My soul and my spirit cry out to you, "Let Him in and say, 'Here I am Lord!'" Jesus loves you. Believe it! At this moment, I cast down any stronghold that plants unbelief, skepticism, doctrines, etc., and allow the Spirit of God to start preparing your heart. I pray for God to send out laborers to bring the Gospel to you. It is God's will to get everyone to heaven. He loves YOU! Love is a magnet. Motivation comes from loving. I pray He is motivating you at this moment.

My children, both young and old, the evil one will always attack your measure of intelligence. He will say, "You are not with it. Oh, you just don't know." How blind THEY are to be so worldly, yet to also miss the leading of the Holy Spirit. You, who have received Jesus Christ as your Lord and Savior, you are the ones who make me happy as I see and watch your spiritual intelligence. To be in tune with the Almighty is, of course, a wonderful gift, and no one seems to understand unless they are in the spirit. What an intelligence! Everything unimportant must fall to the wayside, for the evil one stacks up all kinds of obstacles in your way, sending all kinds of people into your path, and all kinds of educational material that strays one from the word of God. Be not fools. Spend your time studying the word as the Holy Spirit leads, teaches and guides. Be open to the Holy Spirit. Pray each day for His divine guidance.

This cancer chapter has gotten so distracted because this is exactly how the evil one wants it to be. He blocked the time of getting that book from the library. And the county library had so much trouble tracking down that particular book. I now have heard over the television news of the many books stolen or not returned to Pratt Library. Perhaps this is one of them. I'm still going to try to track it down somewhere. But now, back to more in depth study.

The story unfolds gradually: Moth... the destructive character of this insect is used exclusively to illustrate the precariousness and corruptibility of human life. Isa. 50:9, Hos. 5:12, etc., etc. Precarious is defined as dependent on circumstances beyond one's control; uncertain; unstable; insecure; dependant on the will or pleasure of another; liable to be withdrawn or lost at the will of another; having little or no foundation; obtained by entreaty or by mere favor. This mystery that has been written, let those who are in the spirit realize the value for which this has been written. There is the utmost value in this paragraph!

The butterfly is always used as the symbol of life. The word "butterfly" consists of nine letters. The biblical number nine deals with the fruit of the Spirit. The fruits of the Spirit are love, joy, peace, longsuffering, gentleness, goodness, faith, meekness, temperance. All of these temperaments will have a bearing on the healing process of a cancer victim. He must be born again, the tree (man) is made good by the new birth and the good fruit, which is the fruit of the Spirit. Man is not made by doing good; he must have a good heart. He must be born again and then good works will follow. "By grace are ye saved through faith; and that not of yourselves; it is the gift of God; not works, lest any man should boast." (Ephesians 2:8-10). Let his deep mystery in regard to cancer enlighten men who are in tune with the Almighty!

This has been the longest chapter, the most puzzling, flitting from one thing to another just like the moth and butterfly from flower to flower, plant to plant. Every time the cancer message is thought about or tried to be written about, all kinds of forces start their interference, complicating everything. All those in connection with cancer research, or the ailing, must be in unity of deep prayer and life in the Holy Spirit. Seek His help, there is no other way. He is on the throne. He alone will heal and direct man!

Even as I write this, Satan is now trying to put something on me. I can feel vertigo and a slight headache, as well as sickness in my stomach. But immediately I must recognize that this is not natural and I must rebuke it. I am led to move from this place and to pray in the name of Jesus, by the power of His blood and now speak in tongues. As I proceeded to do this spiritually, I saw something like radio waves lifting away from me. I now must follow directions and rest and move from this area.

It is interesting to note at this point the meaning of the number six, being this is the 6th chapter. It is often believed that the number six in the Bible is connected with Satan, the devil and his influence on man, and his evil deeds and false worship. The sixth commandment was "Thou shall not kill." At the sounding of the sixth trumpet, men are found worshipping six false gods. In Luke 17:28, Jesus mentioned six things in connection with the wicked in Lot's time. They ate, drank, they bought, sold, they planted and built, and the same day that Lot went out of Sodom, it rained fire and brimstone from heaven and destroyed them all. There are many more things in the Bible to find and discuss about the number six. I am not speaking of occult numerology, but the genuine word of God, far beyond human capabilities and understanding that was planned, constructed, and formed in every word in the Bible. Praise the Lord!

The Lord led me to watch a television show on moths and butterflies. They showed a picture of the moon and said, "The moon is the navigator for the moths."

Chapter 7
Searching to Understand the Gifts of the Holy Spirit

I continue to study, but at the time, my study group was starting to make several statements through conversations that didn't sit too well with me. One person said he believed that Jesus was probably someone else before he became Jesus, such as Buddha and Moses were. I soon learned that these people believed in reincarnation! This puzzled me, for I knew they belonged to the Episcopal and Methodist churches and said they were Christians. With the ecumenical movement going on, I felt so good that we became so friendly and grew so fond of one another. I felt so very close to all of them. We spent some wonderful days together that will always remain in my memories. Still, I thought, maybe this man only said this as a matter of speculation and didn't really believe it. For many times I would mull things over in my mind and verbally express what I was thinking but not truly believe it. I just passed the whole issue off at that moment.

During that time, a group also started at my home church. I believed this group, too, was a charismatic group who would also be studying scripture and perhaps the gifts of the Holy Spirit. I became very fond of the people in that group as well. It was a very rewarding experience and a great lesson came out of that situation, even though the group disbanded, of which I could not fully understand why. A believing prayer group could overcome anything, in spite of my involvements. Why did anything or anyone hinder this group? I do believe we all had more to learn, but perhaps perseverance and trust were all that were needed to understand the way in which Jesus was using us in His mission. Nevertheless, perhaps in my ignorance, I didn't help any, for I was sharing with the others what was happening in the area of study that I was in. They seemed to relegate me to hell too quickly, not realizing that I was one of God's own who had little or poor teaching in this area. To be an accuser of the brethren is to fulfill the desires of Satan, not God (Rev. 12:10). Someone accused me in that group. I never, for one moment, no longer claimed allegiance to Jesus Christ. How could they be so blind? As a result, I was with Christ and He called me out of that particular group.

One woman in that prayer group spoke in tongues at the prayer meeting. Several days later she told me that the interpretation was that I was contaminating the group. How could they be so blind? The Holy Spirit was my teacher and was allowing me to gain knowledge in this particular area. That always did seem to frighten our people. Of course it was extremely interesting that while allowing me to enter into this study, His hand was always upon me, leading and directing me, keeping me safe from any sinful encounter. Even before I ventured into this so-called area, it was shown to me that I was always protected. This was extremely important to be spiritually aware of that. At this point, I had to be obedient and continue my mission, regardless of what my people thought of me. Deep in my heart, I had hoped that someone in that group really understood and trusted me. There was so much to explain, and I was just too tired from the whole ordeal of life's experience of being in the world of nonbelievers and in the realm of spiritual warfare. Even though I did not fully understand all that was happening, this I did know without a doubt: the Holy Spirit was leading me and had me on this mission.

As time went on, several in each group that I was in began to be at odds with one another. However, the ecumenical group seemed to be into healing and prayer a long time. Then along came the issue of one of the woman's daughters from the church group who was having fainting spells, of which the doctors were not helping the situation. The daughter was also parted from her husband and was about to get a divorce. She was also thinking of going to live with another man. We all, including the mother, prayed with her and laid hands on her in order to stop all of what was about to happen to her. I asked her mother to call us and maybe, through prayer, we could help her.

The next day, we got a call from her daughter asking us to come to her house and pray with her. We traveled to her house and there we laid hands on her and prayed with her. The next day I received a phone call from her mother, who was also present when we prayed for her daughter. She sounded very happy and said that her daughter decided against going to live with the other man. I was so relieved because I did not agree with that kind of set up. It is not in accordance with God's word. Her mother and another friend seemed to hear me mulling this over in my mind and talking out loud, as to how I was thinking of how today's society was thinking in general. At that moment they didn't understand what I meant when I verbally spoke of the feelings of other people as a whole. Satan really got that all mixed up, and they tried to use that particular situation against me at a later time. I guess it really confused my other friend. At this point, through the sincerity of my heart, I want to make this clear: I did not agree with that type of situation, never have and never will. At the time, I was mulling over in my mind what society, in general, was trying to put on our children; that society's thinking was that it was okay. This I know is totally unscriptural. I must also clarify that while I was mulling all of this over, the daughter was not present, just her mother and a friend. So no seeds were planted to confuse the girl. Living together before marriage is wrong!

I was just so happy that she changed her mind and was starting to take some school courses. I, too, believed and was so happy that our prayers helped. Little did we realize another voice entered to talk to the girl. Lo and behold, at a later date, I heard that the daughter did decide to go live with the other man. It was revealed later, from the mother, that some other woman in our study group led her daughter to believe it was the thing that had to be done. I was shocked! I told her mother that at no time did I ever tell her daughter to do so. Her mother then said and mentioned the name of the woman in our ecumenical group that did. I, too, wondered about this woman. I didn't mention this to anyone; I just dropped the issue thinking that in trying to help someone, that woman seemed to mess up the whole thing. But in all honesty, the girl had it in her mind to go live with that man, before she even met the group. So I can't help but believe that she had to lay the blame somewhere and found a place by finding a woman to give her the support. I dismissed it all from my mind because God knew my heart. Things from then on seemed to put everyone at odds with each other. The civil actions were there, but the undertones were taking a different hold. There was much caution and, again, disappointment on my part.

So much began happening at that time. My son and his friends were starting to experience something, but I didn't realize what. I, too, was watching all that was taking place in their lives. I, too, began to study scripture with them. For during a professional performance in New York, while my son was a long distance from home, I began to have moments that something was happening to him. I was not frightened, but felt compelled to call him and tell him of a Prayer House run by Catholic priests and told him to visit there. Something was taking place, for he preferred to stay in, while not playing his music, and read his Bible. His associates couldn't understand this. I found out later that he had visited a Pentecostal church in the area and began to have a personal relationship with Jesus Christ. I couldn't understand this talk, because he was raised a Catholic, attended Catholic schools, went to college prep taught by the Christian Brothers at Calvert Hall and then on to Georgetown University in Washington, D.C. I could not understand all of this, at this time, about finding Jesus Christ as his Lord and Savior. Yes, he knew about Jesus, but this new spiritual awareness was something different. His confirmation was about to take place to really accept Jesus as Lord of his life.

If I am drifting off from one thing to another, it is because that's just the way things were. So many things were happening at once. I was so involved with these three groups: the Catholic Church group, the ecumenical group and my son's group. These people and groups were very close to my heart. However, my son's group had something very special, and I knew the Holy Spirit was leading me to be involved with them. There was the sense of the Holy Presence among them.

I decided to join them in their study, which they found in a United Pentecostal storefront church. I met the minister and his wife and soon realized this was a very learned man who had much influence on these young men. They met for prayer very often and had much fellowship together. My husband and I began to visit very often, to see what the situation was there. At first, I felt relieved that he, at least, was in a Christian atmosphere. After being in college and studying many other religions, he certainly was reading his Bible and finding out that much of the Catholic Church contained man-made laws, which held people in bondage in many areas. He was completely turned off by the ritual and organized prayers and types of celebrations. He was searching for a worship service with the living presence of the Holy Spirit and manifestation of the gifts, as well as a special, personal relationship with Jesus Christ. The organized church seemed no longer his own, for there never was that special awareness time allowed for the Holy Spirit to minister to the body of Christ. Man had it all set up, as to the type of worship it was. Many of the boys in that group then could see that some people were, in a sense, pagan Christians, sacramentalized, yet not having that call to holiness. They saw that many were there through culture and not coming to the fullness of all that Christ had to offer. Many had good intentions, but were missing the whole issue. Many were just stopping at salvation and not moving on to the second experience of the Baptism of the Holy Spirit and the fullness, plus the operation of the gifts of the Holy Spirit. Really, they were searching for something more than they had at their own churches and finally found it in a little Pentecostal storefront church. They immediately felt called to the ministry of music to be used for spreading the gospel. Two of the men in their group felt led this way, but the other boys did not get this leading. It looked fairly dim to look for musicians that were called to do this same thing in this immediate area. But with perseverance, as I will later relate, it did all take place.

Now, getting back to the United Pentecostal storefront church here in town that they found. I began hearing about the issue of Baptism and the way Jesus was baptized. Baptism, I heard, had to be by immersion. I never before questioned any of my Catholic upbringing or the issue in church. I was a child of obedience, I firmly thought, to the church and never questioned those in authority. But as I began to read scripture, I soon realized that something was amiss. I no longer felt everything was in their proper perspective. I could see the value in many things, but they were out of perspective according to scripture. I began to question Baptism, for even at that time, many of my Catholic brothers and sisters in Christ were being re-baptized by immersion. In scripture, I could not find where sprinkling by water is the way Jesus was baptized. Also, he was not baptized as an infant, but that, too, I didn't want to get caught up in. I just listened and heard that so many of our Catholic people were going to other churches and getting baptized by immersion. If Jesus came to show us the way, then why were we not doing as he did??? Every other night I would hear of the many names that were familiar to me, who belonged to the Catholic Church. They were all getting baptized by immersion. I decided to go with my husband to see what was taking place among our youth in the parish, but I would also hear of the many adult members also seeking to be baptized by immersion, and doing so.

In the meantime, the young men of the parish wanted to play some music that they liked at the Catholic Church. This caused much unrest among certain people who only enjoyed the traditional songs. Nevertheless, they were given some leeway and began their songs. We did not realize that one young man was caught up with the Catholics, drinking all night and having B.Y.O.B. (bring your own bottle) affairs at the church. His mother and father drank, and he resented this very much. He even saw people at their church affairs pretty near drunk. One man was so drunk that he could not drive his car home. This all weighed heavily on our youth, so they chose as their communion song, "Be Ready When He Comes." The words that came out loud and clear were, "Don't let Him find you stomping on the bar room floor!" Until this day, I do not believe whether this was completely innocent. I knew that they were totally disgusted with the drinking going on at the church affairs. It certainly caused a great deal of commotion with one woman and her daughter. We all wondered if they, at least, got the message. Her daughter spoke to my son over the phone and said they thought the music was terrible. The woman had a tantrum and had a lot to say. It certainly stirred them up. If only they would realize what was taking place, as far as our youth was concerned. These young people did have much to say, and nobody was listening to what was troubling them in regard to the church. Really, if someone gave these young people some time and effort, they would have something great! They have a message to convey and have much to offer, but first, many of our people have to realize that not everybody likes ballet or classical music. These young people wanted joy in their music.

It would do one good to read Psalm 98: "Sing to the Lord a new song, for he has done wondrous deeds; His right hand has won victory for him, his holy arm. The Lord has made his salvation known; in the sight of the nations he has revealed his justice. He has remembered his kindness and his faithfulness toward the house of Israel. All the ends of the earth have seen the salvation by our God. Sing joyfully to the Lord, all you lands; break into song; sing praise. Sing praise to the Lord with the harp, with the harp and melodious song. With trumpets and the sound of horn, sing joyfully before the King, the Lord. Let the sea and what fills it resound, the world and those who dwell in it; Let the rivers clap their hands, the mountains shout with joy. Before the Lord he comes, for he comes to rule the earth; He will rule the world with the justice and the peoples with equity."

My beloved, be glad and gentle with our youth. They love our Lord Jesus Christ and have found new life in Him and want to joyfully praise and honor Him. Allow them this privilege! In their own way, they want to find the joy that the old church lacked in its own way. Diversity in music, dress, etc. is what makes the world so beautiful. God has so much for us to receive. Who is one to say it has to be to THEIR liking and no other? We do have some high spirited members among us, praise God! Selfish pride causes so much division and strife. Some label it as a "dead Church," and believe me, some are!

In another incident that was really heartbreaking, there were several enthusiastic young men and women wanting to participate in the youth music at the church. They had practiced long and hard on several songs, and on one in particular, these young people spent long hours practicing. In charge was a young man studying for the priesthood, who was not very qualified to work with youth. It was midnight, Christmas Eve, and the liturgy was about to begin. This young up-and-coming priest in charge appeared nervous, and a little while later told the young people to cut out the song that they had practiced so long and hard at. It was such a disappointment to these young people; they lost heart and never played their music there ever again. My heart really went out to those kids, and those in authority handled it all wrong. They really messed up those enthusiastic young people. Thank God they have found refuge elsewhere.

The respect is no longer where it should be, in regard to the church, for they surely did not find love there. A dictatorship, yes, but love and gentle guidance and direction? It just was not to be found there. The church still does not know how to deal with the high spirited. They would rather get rid of them and have the quiet follows who won't say "boo." Programmed, programmed! God has all kinds, and they preach "right to life," which they should! But then deal with all that you have. Don't just get rid of them, which is what they've always done in the past. As they often have said, "They are the bad children." To me they are high spirited and extremely interesting! Praise God!

Well, the drinking still continues in the churches, and some of the youth have copied this terrible habit, causing so much heartache while others, who have come to the light of this, have agonized over it. And those in authority are not doing much about it. I've observed youth hating the church for encouraging this, by having their parents there, and fearing the battles that will take place later on in the home as a result of his. Alcohol is as bad as the drug scene, and there is no excuse in saying it is not. The youth recognize this as a disastrous effect on their generation, and the church is encouraging this by advertising B.Y.O.B. The youth would hope it meant, "Bring your own Bible" instead. There is much prayer going on in regard to this issue. We know we will see results!

As the visits to the United Pentecostal Church continued, my daughter realized that she too wanted to be baptized by immersion. I gently told her that she was baptized, and that it was not necessary. Her heart cried out to be baptized that way. Again and again I did not want to discuss it. Basically, both my husband and I sensed that this seemed very important to our daughter, and something within my spirit told me that Jesus was calling her to be baptized this way. I still battled myself, but deep down I felt very strongly to allow her to go ahead.

Several months prior to all that was happening, I woke my daughter, telling her it was time to get up for school. I went downstairs to make some breakfast for her. It was the same morning that we received a long-distance call from our sister-in-law, telling us that my mother-in-law had just died. That was approximately 4 o'clock in the morning, and I got my daughter up for school at around 7 a.m. She had eaten her breakfast, and we were not dwelling on her grandmother's death. I was just telling her to go to school, and during that time I would pack and we would all prepare to leave for Taylor, Pennsylvania. There had been no tension or anything in regard to all that was happening. It seemed to go well that morning, outside of the sorrow that we all felt for the loss of her grandmother. After she had finished eating her breakfast, she left the table to go upstairs and get dressed. I went to the kitchen sink and started doing the dishes when all of a sudden, I heard my daughter scream a piercing scream. She was very frightened and was running back to me. I quickly took her into my arms to console her and asked what was the matter. She held onto me very tightly and said, "I saw something in the bathroom just as I was coming up the stairway!"

I asked, "What did you see?"

She told me that she saw a face with glowing eyes! I tried to tell her that maybe she was all keyed up about her grandmother and her imagination was running wild. She said, "No, I really saw something, and the eyes were glowing!" As she told this to me, I decided to take her with me and show her that nothing was there. Believe me, I was very cautious. I began to pray as I walked up the steps for I, too, could sense a presence. I also took some blessed holy water with me and prayed in the bathroom and sprinkled some holy water there. Thank God, the fear seemed to go from my daughter, and she went about getting dressed for school.

I dreaded the evening to come, thinking that she would be frightened to go upstairs by herself to bed. I didn't mention anything more about it when she came home. She went about her business as usual. Then came time to go to bed. She went directly upstairs, and I sort of watched in the background, not letting her see me. I saw her go into the bathroom and heard her think out loud and saying, "Yep, it came up right there," pointing to the place where she saw something. She then picked herself up and went to bed. I was so thankful that whatever it was did not leave her afraid. In my other book I will write entitled, *Jessica*, there will be enclosed the sketch of what she saw as she quickly drew it on paper.

At a later date, something in her spirit was crying out to be baptized by immersion. I started to recall that she had been through a great deal. That is a book in itself.

My husband and I both decided, along with her brother, to allow her to be baptized that way. We felt led by the Holy Spirit to allow her to do it this way.

That night, at the United Pentecostal Church, one of which had the necessary type of baptismal for immersion, we also thought, "What harm can be done if this child was dedicating her life to Jesus Christ in this way?" Just as we were getting ready to have her baptized, she came to me and said she saw some creepy faces in the reflection of the store window. She said they were trying to get in to where we all were. She was seeing with the eyes of spirit. We told the minister about it, and he said, "The evil spirits really don't like what is going on and would like to stop all that is about to take place." He said she was seeing into that realm. Nevertheless, my daughter was baptized by immersion and is at peace in this respect. She came out of the water speaking in tongues and baptized in the Holy Spirit. Since then, I can see her under the protection of the Holy Spirit so much. Everyone was so happy for her. Praise the Lord! Since then, most of the problems she had in the past physically, like her anemia and everything, cleared away. At this moment, I feel led to wait with more on this issue in my next book about her.

Soon after that, my children began telling my husband of the importance of baptism by immersion. They had us read about it in scripture and told us about Jesus and the way he was baptized and the way man had changed it. I then remembered the words of John's Revelation Chapter 22:18, 19, "I myself give witness to all who hear the prophetic words of this book. If anyone adds to these words, God will visit him with all the plagues described herein! If anyone takes from the words of this prophetic book, God will take away his share in the tree of life and the holy city described here! Let him who hears answer, Come! Let him who is thirsty come forward; let all who desire it accept the gift of life-giving water." I let all of this take hold of me and said, "Oh, God! I was also baptized in my Catholic Church!" Something led me on further to realize that immersion is the only way to be baptized. I prayed about this, not letting up on prayer. I asked Jesus to lead me and to protect me from getting any unnecessary heartache. Something deep within my spirit was telling me this was the right thing to do, and still I kept battling the issue. Then one evening I planned, in a sense, to go to the church that had the facilities to do the baptism by immersion. Still, I prayed that only if this was the will of God that I would follow through with this.

Soon, the service got under way. They were praising God, singing and praying. All of a sudden I could see, as I closed my eyes, a bright light way off in the distance, slowly coming toward me. It was way off in the clouds, way off in the sky. This was the vision I received. I wondered if this was a figment of my imagination or what??? As I tried to capture more of the vision, the singing and praising began to subside, and slowly everything faded. The preacher then began with the routine of a collection and reading scripture. When that was over, they began to sing and praise the Lord, and all of a sudden again, I could see the vision with closed eyes. That bright light was coming closer, and I finally could make out a hazy picture of Jesus Christ in his white robe slowly coming toward me. I again struggled to question if this was a true vision or whether this was my imagination. Again the singing and praising stopped as they were getting ready for testimonies and praying for different requests, etc., and the vision once again faded. This was a second part, and at this time I go back to one (the number) which symbolizes unity. The meaning here is harmony, peace and fellowship among them. Acts 4:32, "And the multitude among them believed were of one heart and soul." It reminded me that it never fails when God's people are of one heart and one soul, that great power and grace will rest upon them.

VISION IN
UNITED PENTACOSTAL CHURCH
STRUGGLING ABOUT THE ISSUE OF BAPTISM THEN HAD THIS VISION
WHITE LIGHT IN THE DISTANCE COMING TOWARD ME
START
STEP I
QUICK SKETCH
STEP 2 JESUS (HAZY VISION) (BUST FIGURE)
STEP 3 FULL FIGURE OF JESUS CHRIST HOLDING ME AS A LITTLE BABY
(QUESTION AROSE WITHIN MYSELF) WHY WAS HE HOLDING ME AS A BABY IN HIS ARMS???
STEP 4 BAPTISMAL
WATER FOR TOTAL IMMERSION

EXPLANATION 73

BABY BAPTISM???

THE DAY I WAS BAPTIZED BY IMMERSION IN THE NAME OF JESUS CHRIST - TO ME IT WAS MY CONFIRMATION (I TOOK THE NAME JESUS) A LIFE DEDICATED TO MY LORD AND SAVIOR JESUS CHRIST.

BORN AGAIN!

(BURIED WITH CHRIST)

BORN AGAIN!

When Jesus prayed for UNITY of His believers, He was not praying for anyone or those who did not believe or should not believe in Him. UNITY is only possible to those who believe in Jesus. Therefore, this prayer of our Lord cannot be made basic for all the religious bodies regardless of what they believe. Jesus was praying for the unity of those who should believe in Him. This does not mean or embrace the Godless, Christ-denying, Christ-rejecting unbelievers who may hold on to some form of religion or those who have added or taken away from the Holy Word of God.

Then I now ponder on the second part, which brought the vision closer. The number two symbolizes division or separation. When the body is divided into two parts, there is a division or a separation. At this point, I can recall that there was division among the Christ believing churches. Everyone that one would attend would be preaching that truth. They were all so divided, my heart cried out! The body of Christ was being torn apart! I struggled about my Catholic Baptism and yet I told Jesus that I was His and whatever He had me to do, I would be obedient unto Him.

The third part of the service began again with singing and praising the Lord. I closed my eyes once again to close off the world and man who sat next to me, and got my eyes and heart on Jesus. The vision once again came forth as if it were on a television screen, with the hazy bust-like picture of Jesus as if He were doing the leading. I seemed to be aware that I must watch to see what He would do and to follow. The bust-like vision was right in front of me, face to face, then focused on the body of Jesus Christ in His white robe taking me. I then turned into a baby in His arms. He gently carried me over to the Baptismal where He immersed me and told me to follow and be Baptized by immersion. This was all in a vision. There then seemed to be a power over me that there seemed no doubt of what I was going to do. I immediately passed word to the minister that I wanted to be Baptized by immersion. I then did so; I was obedient to His word. It was the most wonderful experience I ever had, to die and be buried with Christ and to be born again! Everything seemed to be complete. I was now ready!

I now ponder over the number three, which symbolizes

Resurrection. Jesus said to His critics, "Destroy this temple, and in three days I will raise it up." I, too, wondered why I saw myself as a baby in Christ's arms, taking me into the water and immersing me. Was this in association with the Catholic belief of the Baptism of infants? Here again, the struggle took place. However, I too wondered why Jesus waited all this time to reveal all of this to me now, as a grown woman. I just knew I had to do it, to be baptized by immersion.

The only upsetting thing in this beautiful, wonderful experience was I wondered how my people of the Catholic Church were going to take my actions in doing this. I knew that I must confess to our Catholic priest all that I had done. At this point, however, it was a matter of being obedient to Jesus Christ and His word, or being obedient to man and the way he had changed this whole thing. I choose, with the Power of the Holy Spirit, to be obedient to Jesus and His word, no matter what the outcome would be. Along with several of our own Catholic boys, we decided to go to our parish priest and tell him what we had done. There was a powerful leading of the Holy Spirit to go and tell.

We then made an appointment to see the priest. We entered the room and told him that we wanted to talk to him about Jesus. We told him what we had done and how we made this commitment of having this personal relationship with our Lord and Savior Jesus Christ. In spite of all that was taking place, we knew that we had done the right thing. Somehow, I couldn't understand why I was crying when I conveyed my message to him. The tears just flowed and flowed, and I couldn't stop them! These tears were similar to another evening that seemed to flow in line with all of this. The tears just came uncontrollably. Yet deep down, I was so very happy and at peace. I truly felt born again! Buried with Christ, I was born again! I then asked the priest if I would be excommunicated. He then said that it was not up to him to say. I really loved my home church, but the Lord himself was now teaching me, and it was as though I was being tested to even leave the church in order to be obedient to the Lord Jesus Christ, to give up and to follow Him! Praise God, Jesus Christ is Lord of my life. I prayed for my people to understand this. Jesus is Lord of my life!

By now the people in my church group did not know how to relate to me, and I'm sure the priests did not either. How could I make them understand when I, too, did not fully understand all that was happening. Yet I sincerely felt and knew that I was being obedient to our Lord Jesus Christ in His leading me into different areas to be on a mission for Him. I know, periodically, He would make His presence known that He was with me. As of now, I was slowly beginning to understand that I was possibly in enemy territory in regard to the other study group. The two young men, my son and our dear friend, Mike D., began to explain that perhaps this group was being mixed up, in a sense, with the understanding of the gifts of the Holy Spirit, because there were counterfeit gifts that the devil gives. I began to start to unfold this terrible mix up by them showing me scripture Deuteronomy 18:10,11.

Perhaps it would be better to start at Deuteronomy 18:9-14. "When you come into the land which the Lord, your God, is giving you, you shall not learn to imitate the abominations of the people there. Let there not be found among you anyone who immolates his son or daughter in the fire, nor a fortune-teller, soothsayer, charmer, diviner, or caster of spells, nor one who consults ghosts and spirits or seeks oracles from the dead. Anyone who does such a thing is an abomination to the Lord, and because of such abominations, the Lord, your God is driving these nations out of your way. You, however, must be altogether sincere toward the Lord, your God. Through these nations whom you are to dispossess listen to their soothsayers and fortune-tellers, the Lord your God will not permit you to do so."

Leviticus 19:31, "Regard not them that have familiar spirits, neither seek after wizards, to be defiled by them: I am the Lord your God." Leviticus 20:6, 27, "And the soul that turns after such familiar spirits, and after wizards, to go a-whoring after them, I will even set my face against the soul, and will cut him off from among his people. A man also or woman that hath a familiar spirit, that is a wizard, shall surely be put to death."

Isaiah 47:9-14, "These things shall come to thee, in a moment in one day, the loss of children and widowhood for the multitude of thy sorceries, and for the great abundance of thine enchantments. Thou art wearied in the multitude of thy councils. Let now the astrologers, the stargazers, the monthly prognosticators, stand up and save thee from these things that shall come upon you. Behold, they shall not deliver themselves from the power of the flame."

Isaiah 8:19, 20, "And when they shall say unto you, Seek unto them that they have familiar spirits, and unto wizards that peep and that mutter: should not a people seek unto their God for the living to the dead? To the law and to the testimony (the word of God): if they speak not according to this Word, it is because there is no light in them." Malachi 3:5,6, "I will be a swift witness against the sorcerers, for I am the Lord, I change not."

At this point I want to thank God, that even in the midst of all of these workshops that were going on all around the college campus, that I was not drawn into a belief in any of these so-called educational areas. I could observe many of what was happening, and perhaps be misled by the so-called spiritual counselors, but at once discerned that this was not Biblical Christianity. But I also thank God for allowing me, while under the protection of His blood, to learn the strategies of the enemy. How deceiving they can be in having people believe that these and their groups were practicing the gifts of the Holy Spirit. At once I recognized that it was the work of the unholy spirit. So many of our people were being caught up in the reincarnation, white magic, E.S.P., astrology, horoscopes, psychics, necromancy, crystal ball gazing, seances, tarot cards, palmistry, numerology, and so many other occult affairs. Little did they realize that delving into these things can sometimes open the door for demon oppression or even possession. Drug and alcohol have the same effect. This can possibly open the door to insanity.

I also found it to be a terrifying thing that this was now being encouraged in some schools. Our children being exposed to E.S.P., evolution, astrology, etc. What we desperately need is to get prayer back into the schools to clear the air around our children! We now must be warned not to study comparative religions, other than Biblical Christianity. "Learn not the way of the heathen, and be not dismayed at the signs of heaven; for the heathen are dismayed at them, thus saith the Lord." Do not let anything be taught your little ones that they would lose their right to the tree of life. There is no such thing as reincarnation. It is just some demons who dwelt in other people in prior centuries, or who dwell in other demon-possessed people now, hovering and oppressing others.

"It is appointed unto men once to die and then the judgment." People today are not aware of the nature of evil spirits. They choose to ignore this portion of God's ministry, and as a result of this, there are great numbers of people living in torment. Much of the ministry of Jesus Christ was devoted to casting out devils of tormented people. We need to know what we are dealing with in each case, hopefully one that is walking with Christ, through the Holy Spirit. He will reveal this to us.

First, the person has to make a whole-hearted personal commitment to Jesus Christ. If a person is not willing to make this commitment, then there can be no permanent solution to his problems. Second, he must be baptized, by immersion, in the name of the Father, Son and the Holy Spirit, and also using the name of Jesus. He must confess to Jesus Christ the sins of one's thoughts, words and deeds, plus any occult involvement, which gave Satan legal access to your life. Third, command with authority that demons go, in the name of Jesus, plead the blood of Jesus and speak in tongues. With all of this, they will flee. Never let your guard down where the enemy is concerned, for he will try in the guise of many different ways to reenter, but you will immediately recognize this and once again plead the blood of Christ, use the name of Jesus, speak often in tongues and soon you will be strong in the Lord. This will not really trouble you so frequently. The only thing for you to look for now is the blessings the Lord will be pouring out to his child. Blessings that seem at times unbelievable!

When oppression is severe, it is advisable to have several born again Spirit-filled believers present, to sing choruses of the blood of Jesus, and only if the person is led by the Holy Spirit to encounter this. Not everyone should attempt this. Demons can attack you also, unless you are truly under the blood of Christ, not just hoping and half believing this. So many times in years past, one would use holy water and many other methods to drive away the spirits, but this would only clear the air for the moment, and it was a hit and miss affair. The demon sometimes got into the person trying to exorcise it, only because, perhaps, the person was not truly born again or a true believer. Remember, a born again child of God has authority over these spirits and should never fear the devil. Command him to leave and he will.

I do not want to go into real depth with this ministry, for this book is not meant to do so in that area. However, I wanted to touch lightly on this, to fully understand my position.

My son, his friend Mike, a few other people, and I read much scripture in regard to all of the new terms that were being used in society today that were confusing people and leading them to believe this was the gift of the Holy Spirit. At this time the churches that we attended were not much help in recognizing the problem among their people by having programs of awareness. In the last days, it is written that even the elect would be deceived. They were just recognizing this. Most of the clergy were being caught up in the whole bad web of destruction, being led by people telling them that they must be up on things. This was the modern world, and sin is no longer. They were twisting and turning everything to suit their selfish needs and were not being obedient to the Word of God. They were changing things to suit the needs of the times, so to speak. That was all well and good, but never in any circumstances should the word of God be changed or any methods that were shown to show the way.

Also during this time, my prayer group at the church, not knowing the full story of why and what I was called to do, was very uneasy with me. Prior to my learning what this scene was all about, I used to share with them that I was studying parapsychology and trying to understand what dreams in that field were all about. I immediately recognized that they were not as friendly as they once were. I couldn't understand why they were like this. It was unbelievable that here was a prayer group, supposedly having the faith and the power of prayer and the knowledge of the Holy Spirit, yet no one was able to come to me to explain what was bothering them. They chose to talk behind my back, making things very uneasy for me. It caused me great sorrow and grief. This prayer group met with some of my people in the study group, and a few of them were really upset with certain people. Yet they could not get it all together to explain what was bothering them. I now realize why. It was because not one of them knew where or how to read it in their Bibles, to show me where it was wrong. They used all sorts of approaches, giving me a book of one of the saints to read, which was helpful, but did not solve the issue. It was a book about St. Theresa; it did comfort me to know that she, too, had supernatural experiences.

There was one in the group who did not know what I was studying, but realized that I was in fellowship with other Christians of other churches. This was a very important issues with me, to really love my other brothers and sisters in Christ, to get to know them better. I respected that one particular woman very much, for she took the time out to visit with me and to try and relate to me that I should do all of my work at my home church, as well as offering me other interesting suggestions. One thing they should realize was that Christ was moving in a new way, and we have to have that spiritual awareness as to where He wants us to be on His mission. There was another young girl in that group, whom I will always respect, who would take time to try to sort out a lot of things by praying with me in regard to the experiences that I tried to share with her. There was also another who would call me to share with me the talks that the others were having in regard to me. She said that she didn't agree with the way they were talking about me. I shall always respect these women who tried to help me understand a section of my life that I had no idea or religious training in, not any teachings in this particular area. It seemed if you would talk about an experience, they would say in a frightened way, "Stay away from it!" I realize they were bogged down by fear. I then thought that I must be very careful and proceed with caution. The important thing was not to be afraid, because I just knew these were the gifts of the Holy Spirit and that we should receive all that God has for us. I was sick and tired of running scared. I was determined to learn the differences between the counterfeit and the authentic gifts of the Holy Spirit. Believe me, it was not easy. Not everyone should attempt it, but with my experiences, I was always shown that I was under the protection of Jesus. But still the learning process was very difficult. I just knew that I was truly under the blood of Christ.

The priest involved wouldn't come up with any answers, so I tried to get them from the various groups of people who were influencing our people in this modern day. This priest would try to understand at times, I really thought, but he never once showed me in scripture where this was wrong. I guessed that maybe he, too, did not know his Bible enough to do so. The only relief that I could get was through my son and his friend, Mike, who had some very good scripture and direction. There was also a man named Neil who came upon the scene, and he was aware of the deception that was taking place among the people in regard to the counterfeit gifts. He decided to take another minister's wife here in town and me down to another church to be prayed over by a spirit-filled minister, and to just talk about things. Prior to that, I still groped for answers from my priest, for so much was happening to our people, including myself. At one point during the conversation, the priest made a statement, "I'm not interested." This was just what Satan wanted, for the relationship to be resolved. I knew deep down that I probably was a terrible thorn in the priest's side, with all of the questioning that I was doing in regard to the areas of study that I was involved in. I couldn't quite understand it all, but deep down I knew Jesus was leading, guiding and teaching me. At the time I couldn't get it all together into words to explain to the church group what this was all about. I had hoped they knew me enough and that they would trust that I was not looking to worship anything or anyone other than the Lord Jesus Christ. Events were taking place in my life and I needed to understand all that was happening.

Nevertheless, as I stated, it was just what Satan wanted. Everyone ran scared and split up. I was too exhausted from being in enemy territory, trying to save souls and leading them to Jesus, plus putting up with the antics of the church prayer group. I was led out of that group by the power of the Holy Spirit.

One night prior to this, during a church prayer meeting, the tears began to flow and flow. I could not stop them. I felt the pain of the suffering souls that were being led astray, and no one was aware or caring just as long as they, themselves, had it all together. They were just content to sit and pray, which in itself is very good, but there was so much happening all around us. Different programs, programs, programs! Works, works! "It is not by works that you are saved," it is written in God's word. Getting the Gospel out and reaching out to the lost seemed so important; time seemed essential. I wondered why, if they thought I was off base, were they not praying for me? They didn't seem caught up with this, and we were supposed to be a prayer group. There seemed to be a lot of talking behind my back.

This was devastating, for I had begun to recognize the counterfeit from the authentic and was starting now to get it summed up in many ways. It helped tie up the loose ends. My son and his friend blessed me, plus with Neil's help, everything came to light and I was getting it together. Thanks to Jesus and His guidance and direction, plus His protection when I would go into areas of difficult learning, especially His protection while in enemy territory, to bring the gospel to those present.

One beautiful morning, I received a phone call from one of the people in the church prayer group asking me to meet her for lunch because she had something to tell me. I had a very busy schedule that day and told her that I could not possibly meet her. I asked her to tell me what happened because she had made the statement that something terrible and devastating had happened to the prayer group, and that it was in regard to me, the cause of it. I then asked her to tell me over the phone, and she then related to me that one of the women at the prayer meeting had spoken in tongues and at a later date went to talk to a minister about the message she received. She was told by the minister that the message was in regard to me and my involvement with my studies, and that I was contaminated and should be prayed over and all the rest who were associated with me. I was contaminated and contaminating others. This was a great disappointment on my part in regard to all of this, my so-called prayer group. I then thought that they were showing a type of religion and denying the power thereof. Why were they not at least praying with me or for me, not adding to my misery? For it certainly was a difficult study to step out on faith to do. How did they know what God was leading me to do? Never once did I get involved in anything that was not of God. I observed many studies, etc., but was always with Jesus Christ and His protection.

The first thing Satan said to me was, "You are contaminated, and there is no helping you. Now go and kill yourself!" For a split second this entered in, and at once I commanded him to go away.

For, thank God, I had already gotten together many questions and the answers. I had already been baptized by immersion, including my daughter and the rest of the family. I knew that I was always under the blood of Jesus, even though I was not brought to the fullness that I now have. I immediately gained strength and felt more disappointment in my church group and their approach to the whole matter. Yes, I can agree that they were on the right track, in regard to someone who was outrightly seeking the counterfeit and that whole ungodly scene. But the shoe did not fit me and I was not going to wear it. I was not going to be accused in that way! Maybe I made some mistakes along the way in gathering my knowledge, but it was all worth it in not having to fear the enemy and knowing the enemy's strategy. But, I cried out, "Why didn't my church prayer group understand and know me better than to accuse me without the facts?" Then the anger began to build again with the disappointment that in such a touching affair, the priest involved didn't have the concern to handle this himself, but chose to have this woman relate the message to me. I only thank God that I was in the strong position with the Lord Jesus, and that at the time I was not driven to do away with myself.

I suffered great disappointment as far as the relationship with the priest. Anger began to build and build, but I recognized that anger was also at Satan. I then fell led to call this woman who spoke in tongues at the prayer meeting, to talk this whole matter over with her and to try to explain my position. Her husband said that she was not in, and he would have her call me back. We waited a long time that evening for her to call back, and in the meantime, my husband and I were becoming impatient and thought her husband should know what was going on too. As my husband related to him just how he felt about the accusation, the husband said it was true, because I did not belong to an organization, the name of which he had mentioned. Little did he know what my mission was, and in judgment, he made this uncalled for accusation which caused a lot of heartache and turmoil. It certainly was not the approach to be taken without the whole story told, that of which I would have been happy to tell if it were asked of me, especially if I was also connected with the church group. But everyone was forming his or her own opinions without the true story in the light of Christ. Well, that woman never called back, after several attempts to get in touch with her. My husband called back a few times, telling him that if this talk continued in regard to me, he would get a lawyer to deal with this. The husband seemed to hold his position about my involvements, as if he ever spoke to me about this, which he never did. In fact, he did not know me very well, outside of a casual acquaintance through church attendance. He really did not even know me and I wondered who was telling him and his wife of my other involvements. This all seemed preposterous! Something was afoot, and I did not like it at all. And this is what you would call our prayer group?

I must mention this couple was from Germany. At this time I couldn't help but wonder if they really were in Jesus Christ, to condemn me without bringing me the gospel to be sure I had the proper teaching on whatever issue they seemed to be caught up with in regard to me. It disappointed me and showed me to actually be a witness as to how they handle a situation such as this. They would knock a person down with their approach rather than through prayer and proper teaching first. The convicting approach should have been last. It was too complicated an issue to be told. Why did they not trust me? I kept asking that question. Why did they not trust me and believe me? I had my hands full on this mission that was affecting my daughter and a whole lot of other things. Since this woman and this particular husband did not try to contact us in any way, it reminded me of Germany and all of its "destroy the imperfect!". All kinds of thoughts were waving in, but I finally rose above it all.

I then decided they could think what they wanted because I knew where I stood in regard to our Lord Jesus Christ and that nothing anyone said or will say would bother me. The important thing here was that God knew what this whole mission was all about. I felt at peace where I was. I knew the Lord led me in this venture and I was not going to worry about any one of them in what they were saying. I no longer felt led to go back to that particular prayer group. Even before all this happened, for some reason I felt the Lord calling me out of that particular group. To be honest about it all, I knew that one woman there was like a roaring lion every time that I was in her presence at the prayer group. You couldn't find a nicer person on the surface, but something inside her was terrible. I could always sense it. I must add that this was not the woman that spoke in tongues against me. I must be careful not to reveal which one it was, because that was revealed only to me just to know of her. As time goes on, it is all proving itself. I knew it was in order to break off a relationship that had started to develop. I just couldn't put my finger on what it was, but I have shelved it for future reference and slowly it is revealing itself. She certainly comes forth as being an angel of light, but the undertones that I discern is "watch out"!

I know now Satan was out to destroy that particular prayer group and their relationships. Basically speaking, it could have been a great one if things were handled in the right way. It could have been one of the best! But, everyone scattered in fear rather than getting everything together.

I know now that Satan was out to destroy that prayer group's relationships, and as of now, he has succeeded with some. Everyone seemed to run in fear instead of taking the authority over this and demanding that this spirit depart. I don't believe anyone at this time knew enough to handle it all, including myself. So much was happening to each of us, in our own realm, that we had little time or energy to handle what was happening to our prayer group. In spite of all that happened, I do believe it was a growing experience for many of us. Instead of gathering together, we went our separate ways. Still, growing and living a life in the spirit was not readily understood. Especially important was to have those who were dear to you understand the mission that our Lord had for each one of us when, at times, we ourselves did not fully understand; but we did step out in faith to follow and be obedient. It gave me an opportunity to be concerned about what my friends or those in authority were thinking about me, but more important, I was not to grieve away the spirit.

During the upheaval of the incident with my church prayer group, the other study group gave me much comfort and consolation. At that time, I didn't know that many of the studies of this group going on were not in accordance with the true gifts of the Holy Spirit, as was often spoken. Once receiving the Baptism of the Holy Spirit, everything began to sort itself out. I recognized

Holy Spirit. John and Mike taught only by using scripture as it is written, through prayer and authority. Neil, through prayer and scripture, but also through his spirit-filled man, lay hands on me for prayer. Through their gentle love and guidance that shed so much light on all that was taking place. These people had a great bearing in my life by solving these issues and having victory. It was through love, gentle teaching, prayer, but most of all by reading the Bible. Thank God for His word! It was not by bickering, accusations, fear and abandonment that these matters were resolved, and especially not by dictatorship! For you see, all my life, I have been dealing with the aspect of love. It was the way my mother and father dealt with me. It was always in love. This, of course, was the only way in which I would respond to anyone.

I have no regrets, even now, because this experience was a learning one that really taught me to rely on God alone and not on man, through the leading of the Holy Spirit. I really came out of this thinking, "Wow! I'm really a child of God! He did watch over me and guide me through all of this. His hand was always upon me." It really gave me the confidence to forge ahead, no matter what kind of mission he delegated to me. This area seemed to have everyone running in fear and it has always been that way. We were told to never talk about things like Satan, etc., but all along we have the victory in Jesus Christ and no longer have to run in fear. The fear is what scattered His people, and they still remained scattered, but perhaps at this time, at this moment, we all have learned a great deal from this experience. God is now using all of us in different places and in many different ways.

All of my fear and burdens were lifted once I found victory in Jesus, and the counterfeit was recognized. It was unbelievable! As I mentioned, there were always effects around. When encountering this scene, one must always be prepared. Of course, it is having a spiritual awareness that we can counteract it. Knowledge in the gifts of the Holy Spirit verses the counterfeit, first of all, is acquired when one is under the blood of Jesus. This can be disastrous if one is not. Many dealings must be dealt with in pure love, agape love, and the way Jesus meant it to be. So much has been accomplished in this way.

One thing to note is that Satan's love is perverted and lustful.

Chapter 8
The Church Prayer Group Number 1

Perhaps I should start with... that as I write all of this in love and sometimes for us all to grow, we have to face reality in the projection of... this is the way it was!

It was a strong group, but it lacked the true love of Jesus Christ. We had something very good going, but there was an undertone that was not right. I guess it was a very good beginning, but the way things were handled could have led to disaster. I can now fully understand how an acquaintance, who shared with me that she had some problems, went to discuss them with another priest and the so-called Christians. I can now understand how she later went and threw herself in front of a moving car and tried to kill herself. These are delicate situations where Satan immediately gets into a situation. People are groping with what is happening to them, and unless this is handled as Jesus would have handled it, it can be very dangerous. There was a great lesson to be learned here. Christ is always the victor, so why was this group so afraid? They were running in fear. I still love them all and have great concern for each one of them, in spite of the added heartache they caused. In love, I must not mention names.

As it appeared to me, there was a great deal of secrecy among the prayer group members, who judged situations that they knew nothing about, in respect of knowing God's leading through the Holy Spirit. Some of the members were handling the situation of my involvements very well. I, of course, love them dearly and respect them very much. I mention no names because as I have written previously, this is the way this all appeared to me. Everyone was doing their best, I'm sure, and I still love them all and have great concern for each one of them, in spite of all the added heartache they caused me.

One member disturbed me very much. It seemed that every time I was near her, I could feel something like a roaring lion inside her. I couldn't understand it, but was led not to have much association with her, even though the Christ in me still loved her. The Lord is revealing to me at this later date what that was all about. I could sense something inside her and I feared to question what. At a later date, I found out that she had cancer. I did not quite understand it all at the time of my association with her and I did not delve to know. It was revealed at a later time.

There were several people that turned me off because they felt so exclusive. Other fellow Christian brothers and sisters would visit and the reception was not too much of love, but of suspicion. Yes, they were civil, but love??? That was questionable. The calls that would come the following day from my own church group in regard to these people who were visiting. My people in the church prayer group, certain ones, did not sound like born again Christians speaking. It was very disheartening. I felt very disappointed in the effect that this was a prayer group that was to have faith in the power of prayer and not cast any away until the gospel was presented to them. Instead, they were running scared. This was the purpose of the prayer group, I thought, certainly to change these thoughts and things that were leading our people astray. There just was no unity, which I had been searching for. It was a matter of accusation and dictatorship, rather than a gentle leading and teaching. Sometimes, they were very harsh, especially when I was questioning and searching and being told, "I'm not interested, specifically in areas much to my concern.

This statement should never have been used because it was just what Satan wanted and used to bind any further contact with that priest. Every time I would want to discuss anything or go to confession, I would hear the words, "I'm not interested." It bound me, at that moment in time, as much as I would like to talk and explain things to this priest. I am still bound. I have been praying about this, but the Lord through the Holy Spirit leads me to believe that the priest has to make the first move. Where, or if, that ever happens will be up to him. The statement came from him, and it is for him to get rid of it, I am told. In spite of all that happened, I truly saw him as a brother in Jesus Christ and respect him very much.

Satan, perhaps, used another member of the prayer group through the way that she handled the message in tongues to accuse me of different issues. Satan is an accuser. God, through the Holy Spirit, does not work that way. Satan saw this prayer group starting and entered in to break it up in the best way he could, by oppressing us. One must be spiritually aware to recognize these tactics. Everyone seemed to flee in fear. One difficult thing was that the people involved did not recognize the many ways the Holy Spirit was using us by leading us into different situations, where there was work to be done. All that they recognized was not good; they did not see the plan of God unfolding. This disappointed me very much and rather than cause any more problems with my involvement, the effect that it had on them and the reasons for it, I decided to pull out of the prayer group.

In anger and in love, the struggle was there. It really was very complicated for me to try to explain all that was happening. God knew my heart and there were leadings from the Holy Spirit that I, myself, did not fully understand at that moment. In love, I didn't want to subject them to any of my involvements. I knew that I had to trust in the Lord, because He was teaching me so many things in so many ways. But the group was bound by fear where I was concerned. It was not easy, for the many situations and involvements were exhausting me and causing me great distress! I was very tired of being in enemy territory. It was very disturbing, and the effects would sometimes take their toll. I couldn't put up with the effects of the payer group; it was all too much to handle at this moment. I resolved by the kind leading of the Holy Spirit to rely totally on God and praise God. He was the only one that got me through all of this, with the best teaching that I would ever get. It was just wonderful the way the Lord was allowing me to work all of this out with the freedom and love. His hand was always on me, gently guiding and protecting me. One truly had to be under the blood of Jesus to even attempt this area of learning.

The people He used constructively were John, Mike and Neil, none of whom were in that church prayer group, but were certainly brothers in Christ who were spirit-filled. I thank God for them everyday, for God used them in a way of love that tied up the whole matter of bringing me to understanding the fullness of the

Holy Spirit. John and Mike taught only by using scripture as it is written, through prayer and authority. Neil, through prayer and scripture, but also through his spirit-filled man, lay hands on me for prayer. Through their gentle love and guidance that shed so much light on all that was taking place. These people had a great bearing in my life by solving these issues and having victory. It was through love, gentle teaching, prayer, but most of all by reading the Bible. Thank God for His word! It was not by bickering, accusations, fear and abandonment that these matters were resolved, and especially not by dictatorship! For you see, all my life, I have been dealing with the aspect of love. It was the way my mother and father dealt with me. It was always in love. This, of course, was the only way in which I would respond to anyone.

I have no regrets, even now, because this experience was a learning one that really taught me to rely on God alone and not on man, through the leading of the Holy Spirit. I really came out of this thinking, "Wow! I'm really a child of God! He did watch over me and guide me through all of this. His hand was always upon me." It really gave me the confidence to forge ahead, no matter what kind of mission he delegated to me. This area seemed to have everyone running in fear and it has always been that way. We were told to never talk about things like Satan, etc., but all along we have the victory in Jesus Christ and no longer have to run in fear. The fear is what scattered His people, and they still remained scattered, but perhaps at this time, at this moment, we all have learned a great deal from this experience. God is now using all of us in different places and in many different ways.

All of my fear and burdens were lifted once I found victory in Jesus, and the counterfeit was recognized. It was unbelievable! As I mentioned, there were always effects around. When encountering this scene, one must always be prepared. Of course, it is having a spiritual awareness that we can counteract it. Knowledge in the gifts of the Holy Spirit verses the counterfeit, first of all, is acquired when one is under the blood of Jesus. This can be disastrous if one is not. Many dealings must be dealt with in pure love, agape love, and the way Jesus meant it to be. So much has been accomplished in this way.

One thing to note is that Satan's love is perverted and lustful.

It is interesting to watch and note the way in which some people will reject that kind of love, but will relate always to the kind of pure love that Jesus had. There are only times when Satan has certain people spiritually blind to have them think that his kind of love is that one kind, and one wouldn't enjoy anything else. Satan's love is only temporary and really not fulfilling, but the Christ love is only the everlasting kind and complete in every sense.

As I stated before, this prayer group is only my view of the whole matter and in the way it all came across to me. Basically there were some good moments and at times some very good teaching there, but there was always the disturbing undertones of one person there who used others to do her wicked things and looked very innocent by herself. The Spirit showed me this very clearly. There were moments of beautiful silence and prayer, and probably it would have been one of the best prayer groups to be had, as well as something very good and very powerful. It really got very heavy for several of us, and perhaps this was a time of getting things together, to rely solely on God, not man or each other.

This, to me, was the whole gist of the lesson there. The isolated moments of being all by myself for a time, God took hold of me and sorted it all out. He held me together. He loved me, for I could feel His love, even at the darkest moments. He gave me confidence that He understood why I was involved in the areas that I had been in, because He was doing the leading and He knew my heart. As a final result, I had found victory in Jesus Christ. The book explains much, as to the reasons of my many involvements. It certainly was not that I was searching for something, but because of what had entered into my life, I was seeking to understand the manifestation of the gifts and in my own way with the leading and guidance of the Holy Spirit to have victory. As I look back, it is very rewarding that through it all, I don't feel that I was ever drawn into sinning, as some in my prayer group thought. God would lead me always away from the areas that were not of Him and into the areas of teaching that were of Him. Sometimes, He would allow me to observe and I thank God for that! I hovered over areas in this learning experience, but never really go involved. I always had my eyes and heart on Jesus Christ. Praise God! He protected me. Even in my ignorance, I seemed to always be under His protection. He kept teaching me to receive all that He had to offer, yet showed me the so-called counterfeit.

Even now, at times, there is a hovering while I am trying to complete this book. It is so wonderful to be able to recognize when it is not of God and to rebuke it in the name of Jesus. It seemed that the counterfeit does not want this book in print. He always tries to put a dizziness over me, to confuse me while I am typing, but there is victory in Jesus and the power of His blood.

There came a time of total silence, peace and solitude, after that experience with the first church prayer group. It was a time to be alone with my Lord and myself. A peaceful time! I still loved those who were involved, yet kept at a distance. God is still working, or perhaps this episode has come to an end, and it is now all in the past. All things become new; old things are passed away.

It sure was an experience. Fear seemed to permeate this group. I experienced a severe loss of energy at times. A certain person present there seemed to drain me of my energy. I couldn't explain it at the time, but as time went on, I found out that she had cancer and perhaps the vibrations that I was picking up at the time were taking their toll. We did not know that this cancer was there at the time. Perhaps this explains why I felt a loss of energy, for until I was able and learned to turn all the burdens over to Jesus, I would feel the infliction that people had. It was terrible. I felt at a loss when people asked for prayer, for it seemed that when I would pray for them, I would feel and take upon myself their sickness or pain. It was not until I learned to pray for them, but turn it all over to Jesus as he said, "Give your burdens to me." All glory and honor is His. We often try to take the credit, but the glory only belongs to Him, leading in our lives. It was not until I got rid of self that I could properly pray for our brothers and sisters, and not experience their pain and suffering. Then also by His leading of the Holy Spirit, that I could then know what and how to pray for someone. Sometimes, it was not an easy matter.

This prayer group is the most difficult to explain in more detail, as I go over and over this written work. I hope that I've shed some light on all that had happened.

It is now extremely important that I ask and pray about certain prayer groups and groups of good works. It is the most unusual, but there are many prayer groups and good works going on, which often invite me to participate, but before I enter, I must be spiritually aware of where the Holy Spirit is leading and wants me to be. Many times, I am about to join a group and the Holy Spirit says, "No, not here." I then must be obedient and not get ahead of Him, but wait for His leading.

Before closing this episode in my life, I must bring forth that in the very beginning, with the eyes of the Spirit, I seemed to see Jesus calling me out of this particular prayer group. I was not obedient at that time, for I really couldn't understand why Jesus would be calling me out of a prayer group. I struggled to understand why and then thought that maybe it was the devil calling me out of the group, because I understood he did not like to see prayer groups functioning, for it cleared the air of the demonic spirits. Even after a time, I could sense a presence, which I realized was Jesus. He seemed to tap me on the shoulder and say, "Come, follow me." I struggled and questioned whether or not this was of Jesus or my imagination. It was awesome!

As time went on, as everything in its time unfolded, I could see the hand of God in my life. If only I were obedient, I could have avoided all that heartache. As I now advance forward, I am truly following the leading of the Holy Spirit in my life, in every area. I have now come to the fullness of the Holy Spirit. I have responded to "Come, follow me"! It was through a thorough searching, of giving all to Jesus. He even dealt with me at times to see if I would give certain things up for him, all possessions, that of which He later revealed to me was not what he wanted. It even came to the realm of the Catholic Church, that of which He too wanted to be given up. After a terrible struggle, I could even say "yes" in that respect. That, too, is was not what he wanted of me. It's ironic, the testing that He put me through to see if I would give up all for Him, to put Him first above anything and everything. Even my family, I had to give all to Him. But the beautiful part of it all was that it was a pleasure to do so. Jesus is first in my life. Seek first the kingdom of God and all these things will be added onto you. It wasn't simple. The testing was great, and God knew my heart. He knew if I was sincere or not. Jesus is Lord of my life! He knew it, and the adventure has now begun through the power and leading of the Holy Spirit. Life is exciting and beautiful, fulfilling beyond one's imagination. Praise God! Everyday is an adventure, but until death, I must be spiritually aware, for the counterfeit is always plotting to get your soul. Stay close to Jesus and walk with him in prayer and fellowship with believers, true born again believers. Read the word often, for it is through the word and His leading, through the Holy Spirit that we will have the keeping power of Jesus Christ. Receive Him in the Holy Eucharist.

Chapter 9
The Study Group... All Faiths Combined

This started out as a very interesting group. The gifts of the Holy Spirit were being studied, along with many other interesting topics. It was a very intellectual group. It was also a very close-knit group with much love and very strong-minded people. It was always an interesting evening, with much fellowship, along with study. It was always very well done and in good taste.

The meetings would always start out with a prayer, especially to St. Michael, the Archangel, for protection. Many of the gifts of the Holy Spirit would be in operation, however as I look back with the knowledge that I now have, I can see where it was marbleized with, perhaps, the counterfeit. It started out very good, but as time when on, there were people who came in that were off base. Also, as I began to study scripture, I could plainly see through the leading of the Holy Spirit, that there was error in place here. As time went on, Satan seemed to get a foothold, and many undesirable things began to happen. Verbal fighting seemed to take place among two people, which led many involved to become discouraged, and there came a split. I also left the group when I recognized the counterfeit there in places.

I tried to remain for a period of time, constantly witnessing for Jesus Christ, His Word, and the gifts of the Holy Spirit. It just didn't register with some, but praise God, a few responded to His word and did come out through my witnessing. Many of the counterfeit schemes did not come out at the meetings for a very long time. Satan really knows what he is doing. Scripture was often quoted, so therefore the average person would not suspect there was error here. It looked so right, yet I was always cautious, for I could feel something in the air that sometimes left me very restless and tired. It was ironic, too, because it looked so safe, for there were so many ministers and sometimes priests involved, too.

Gradually, as time went on, a speaker was scheduled to speak and lead the program for the evening. He was supposed to be an ordained minister, which seemed in proper order. However, that evening he was present, I decided to use scripture where in 1 John 4:1-3, it tells us how to test the spirits. "Beloved, believe not every spirit, but try the spirits whether they are of God, because many false prophets are gone out into the world. Hereby know ye the Spirit of God: Every spirit that confesseth that Jesus Christ is come in the flesh is of God; And every spirit that confesseth not that Jesus Christ is come in the flesh is not of God; and this is that spirit of the antichrist, whereof ye have heard that it should come; and even now already is it in the world." After this minister spoke in far out areas and seemed very puzzling at times, he asked if anyone had any questions. I then said, "Yes, I have one." I asked him if he believed that Jesus Christ died for our sins. He than started a whole spiel, and in trying to get him to say a "yes" or "no," he finally said, "No." Immediately, a red flag went up for me, and I realized that this man was a false prophet and that I should not absorb anything that he was saying and should be very cautions. Many other things started to take place, such as he began to read foreheads. Yes, not palms, he read foreheads, which seemed to be quite a switch from the counterfeit occult reading of palms.

It was all supposed to be for fun, and I soon realized that much of the so-called fun was leaning toward the occult. It was nothing serious, but fun games. I see now that it was probably Satan's way of getting his edge in. Many of our people were also taken in by horoscopes, astrology, etc. Beware. It is a tool of the devil to slowly but surely take you in by all of these things. Do not let the stars guide your life; let Jesus through the Holy Spirit. God said, "I am your Lord, thy God, thou shall have no strange gods before me." Jesus Christ is Lord. Look unto the Holy Spirit to lead your life. Nothing and no one else should! There were also remarks made about reincarnation, dead people coming to several in the spirit through people they know, etc. It was coming from several so-called Christians that they did not really believe Jesus was always Jesus, but that He was Moses, Buddha, etc., until reincarnated into Jesus. This all began to turn me off completely, especially reading from Holy Scripture, Deuteronomy 18:10-12. "There shall not be found among you anyone that maketh his son or daughter to pass through the fire, or that useth divination, or an observer of times, or an enchanter, or a witch, or a charmer, or a consulter with familiar spirits, or a wizard, or a necromancer. For all that do these things are an abomination unto the Lord; and because of these abominations the Lord thy God doth drive them out from before thee."

I thank God for the written word when in doubt as to whether we are to receive all that He has for us. The selfish desires of some present led them to disregard the scripture. I fear for them, for they have been witnessed to and yet are still in bondage to all of these so-called fun games. I still pray for them, however at this time, I am told by the Lord not to exert any more energy for them. It is now their decision. I still pray, though, that the Lord will reach them. Yet with themselves blocking the light with their selfish self, they many not open themselves up in faith to our Lord Jesus Christ. Time will tell. My love is still there for them all, yet I am so limited to what else I can do. I have laid hands on them and prayed for them, yet only on a few of them, because I know that there is a strong foothold by the others who are blocking some of them from coming fully to Christ. Some have made it, yet some are at the brink, and some I can see Satan really blocking them and having them bound. It is all up to themselves whether or not they get under the blood of Jesus Christ, as to whether they will be saved or not. Once they do get under the blood of Jesus, Satan will flee, but until then, they are bound. He remains!

I am led, at times, to pass on information that is verified by Holy Scripture. However, they have made it known that they do not believe in scripture and have no faith. It is so heart breaking, because there is no sense in trying to talk to such people. All the talking in the world will do no good. It is now time to take complete authority over them, in the name of Jesus, and deliver them. Satan has a stronghold over them and won't even allow them to go up for prayer. Deliverance is the only answer Authority and victory! The only obstacle is when and where this should be done. Those of us who are interested will be shown how and where.

Several spirit-filled people observing these people have

discerned evil spirits around these people, seeing with the eyes of the spirit. In particular, one minister is involved in practices that God has forbidden and was in a terrible state of health, and at that point was willing to try anything. But Satan still had him bound by keeping him interested in things of occult nature. Even though he consented to be prayed over and baptized by immersion, it seemed that he was trying anything. But I wondered if this baptism was really from the heart and his being repentant for his occult involvements. Was he going through the motions of praying to Jesus Christ, etc., yet not really believing that Jesus is his Lord and Savior? I wondered how God was looking upon this man. I continued to send pamphlets with teachings in regard to all of his involvements, verified by scripture. I never got any response, so I don't really know what, if any, impact was there. He lived very far away, and after writing several notes with no answers from him, I really don't know what happened to him in the end. He died of cancer. Perhaps more information will come in, for one of the group was scheduled to make a trip to that area and was finally going to talk to an aunt that had taken care of him in his final days. At a later date, this young man came back, but I, as of yet, have not been able to talk with him about this minister in his last days.

Prior to all of this, there is one consolation well remembered. One evening while having a social evening, the Holy Spirit revealed to me that evil spirits were tormenting him. I could see them hovering over him. They looked animalistic and would, at times, superimpose over him as he sat in the chair. Seeing with the eyes of the spirit, God was revealing this to me. I then told him what I was seeing and soon asked him if he wanted to be prayed over. He said "yes" and consented to this. And as the Holy Spirit led, it was leading toward this minister to ask him if he would be baptized by immersion. He decided that he did want this done; he seemed desperate. This baptism did take place. It really was an event with this minister's baptism. In spite of him being baptized in the church by sprinkling, his spirit seemed to realize that he must be baptized by immersion, a sign of obedience to our Lord Jesus Christ. There were two of us there who realized and confirmed with his spirit that this had to be done. He, too, agreed but I really don't know if this was from his heart or if he was just reaching out for anything, knowing he was dying of cancer. As a Catholic and hazily realizing that I could baptize if death were imminent, I asked him if he would like me to call a pastor to arrange this kind of baptism. He said, "No, I want you to do it." This was a serious matter and unless you were in the spirit, it would seem so ridiculous, even hilarious.

There were four women present and the owner of the house was told to fill her bathtub full of water for a baptism by immersion. The minister was then given a yellow sheet to wrap himself in. He was such a large man, but nevertheless, he was immersed and baptized in the name of Jesus... the Father, Son and the Holy Spirit. A power seemed to overtake the room and all flowed very smoothly. It's ironic, but as I was baptizing him, he seemed to look like a baby there for a split second. Once again, the baby issue came about when the baptism occurred, just like when I saw Jesus at the time of my baptism by immersion. Jesus held me in his arms, and for a split second I, too, was a baby. This all needs to be prayed about, for I feel and see Jesus trying to convey a message here to us.

No matter how things ended for the minister, as one gentleman said, "At least he was immersed in baptism like Jesus instructed us to do." Praise God! Many prayers using the name of Jesus Christ were said over him. Whether this was done from the heart, God only knows. Time will tell, I thought.

The next page shows a quick sketch of the kinds of evil, animalistic spirits that were always hovering around him.

At a later date, I once again was in the minister's presence, prior to his leaving to live with his aunt. As I carefully listened to his conversation, lo and behold, there he was talking about things of the occult. I was utterly disappointed and realized that he was not totally dedicated to Jesus Christ, because all these things were an abomination to him. Perhaps all that baptism, etc., was really not from the heart. I knew then that it all was not going to work, for he was truly not repentant in these areas. Yet, I had to keep working beyond this point, which I did. Being so far away made things very difficult to know whether or not he really accepted Jesus Christ as his Lord and Savior and was delivered. Certainly

ANIMALISTIC
EVIL SPIRITS
THE MINISTER

many prayers were sent up for him. The only hope of any information was when our friend would visit the aunt. As of now, while I am writing this, there is still no word.

One amazing fact is that while attending a Full Gospel Businessmen's Prayer Fellowship one evening, this minister's name came to me during the intercessory prayer time, along with the words, "Deliver him, O Lord!" I didn't realize what that was all about, but I thought about it. That was Saturday evening, and the following evening I received a phone call. A woman friend told me that the minister had died. It is my hope and prayer that all of those people at the Full Gospel Businessmen's Fellowship praying the prayer, "Deliver him, O Lord," helped. I wish to remember that prayer of deliverance and wish to remember him that way. It was over, and hopefully peace was there with him.

Still another incident with one other person in that group was that she, too, was experiencing terrible upheavals in her life, not realizing that her involvements with these so-called spiritual counselors and dabbling in the occult were bringing in these evil spirits to hover around her. She would often come to me when she would feel this awful, rough time. I soon recognized that this terrible evil, animalistic spirit was also superimposing itself over her periodically. I described this to her, and she confirmed that was exactly what she would see coming at her. It was terribly frightening to her. I began to pray with her, telling her that she had to step out in faith and receive Jesus Christ as her personal Lord and Savior and to get under the blood of Jesus Christ. At that time of desperation, she, too, was willing to do anything. However, I wondered and questioned if this was all from the heart. This terrible spirit seemed to leave her after praying with her. I still kept praying for her, for something within my spirit led me to watch and see if, at a later date, that she really meant it. She, too, seemed to stay with a great deal of the belief in reincarnation, etc., which led me to be very cautious when around her. She, too, was in need of deliverance.

I was led to continue to pray for her, read scripture in regard to the things she was involved with that were an abomination to our Lord. I was led to taper off our relationship, only to periodically meet her, always witnessing for Jesus Christ. There for a while,

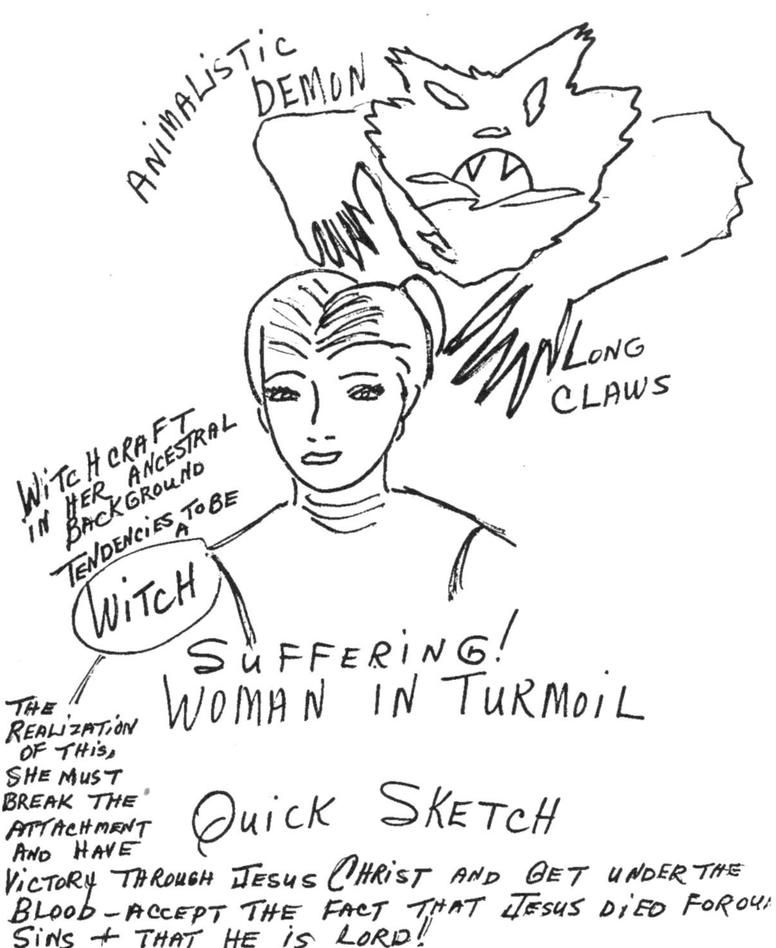
ANIMALISTIC DEMON
LONG CLAWS
WITCHCRAFT IN HER ANCESTRAL BACKGROUND
TENDENCIES TO BE A
WITCH
SUFFERING!
WOMAN IN TURMOIL
THE REALIZATION OF THIS, SHE MUST BREAK THE ATTACHMENT AND HAVE
QUICK SKETCH
VICTORY THROUGH JESUS CHRIST AND GET UNDER THE BLOOD - ACCEPT THE FACT THAT JESUS DIED FOR OUR SINS + THAT HE IS LORD!

she would often be led not to come to meet us. I could sense the spirit within her, rejecting Jesus Christ as her Lord and Savior. Then again, when she would feel this terrible torment, she would seek me out to pray with her to clear the air around her. I recognized that she was in a terrible spiritual battle. It was exhausting for me to be around her at these times. There seemed a draining of my own energy. I soon came to realize that this was a job to be done by someone other than myself, and through the Holy Spirit's leading, I am no longer led to exert any more energy where she is concerned. I am called out of this situation, for the time being. What the next step will be, at this point I know not. This, I do know. There has to be deliverance. By whom? Time will tell. There seemed to be more evil spirits hovering around her husband, of which I was not capable of handling. Things have been left up in the air as to what my next encounter will be with them.

So many others were being misled into thinking that these were gifts of the Holy Spirit in operation, yet mixed up with the counterfeit. Many came out of this scene without any hesitation, after reading scripture and sorting out the authentic with the counterfeit. Yet so many others were already oppressed and would not budge. Those of us who saw the light tried desperately to get through to them, but there seemed to be a wall of evil spirits all around them. Deliverance with authority was needed to be done to get the victory, and this was not to be done by myself. I wondered at this time who and where the Holy Spirit would lead. At this point, I wish I could complete this for you. Perhaps before I complete this book, I may have some more information regarding this matter.

So many of the people have come out of this terrible mix-up, praise God, yet so many are still being tormented. One other girl has terrible moments too often, and they are also caused by a hovering evil spirit, and only a spirit-filled person can recognize this. One evening, with the eyes of the spirit, I could see this evil spirit superimposed over her at times. It just stared at me, very frightened, yet just staring and staring. I commanded it to leave her in the name of Jesus Christ, spoke in tongues and pleaded the blood of Jesus. It seemed to leave and then come back, off and on again. I continued to keep praying and finally was led not to give it any attention. Then it seemed to leave. I no longer paid any attention to seeing it that evening, but I soon realized these certain people were all attracting these terrible evil spirits, and there was one huge one for each of them. They were in dire need of deliverance. It was also made known to me that it was not for one single person to attempt deliverance for these people, but a great number of believers in Jesus Christ who were spirit-filled.

After praying for this woman, she did feel better, but I knew this was not the end of all this torment for her. She needed to repent and commit her life to Jesus Christ from her heart, not just something to do on the surface, but to also reject any occult involvements, if any.

The husband of this woman seemed the most oppressed. I could see with the eyes of the spirit, an evil spirit much different from the rest. This was a human-like, huge satanic form that hovered over him, not letting anyone get through to him. The other evil spirits seemed more animalistic. If this make a difference, I really don't know. However, this man with the human form, satanic spirit, seemed more oppressed than the others. He had no faith at all to step out in faith and accept the Bible as the word of God. The others, under comparison, neither accepted nor rejected scripture, where this man totally rejected the entire Bible. I could see this terrible huge satanic black figure blocking him completely.

At this point, I invited him to a full Gospel Businessmen's Fellowship dinner, to have him hear a minister speaking on the occult and its dangers. But he seemed to stay until the end of the talk, then left quickly after the affair was over. I did not have any time to talk to him and find out what he thought of the whole evening. The evening was very informative, I thought, but there should have been a deliverance type of prayer to complete the evening, for many left oppressed. Victory should have been taken over all that was said. There in the body of true, spirit-filled people, there would have been a fantastic deliverance service there. But perhaps the Holy Spirit did not choose this evening, for there were a great deal of unbelievers who were not under the blood of Jesus Christ, and the so-called evil spirits would have had a ball jumping from one to the other.

QUICK SKETCH
SPIRIT
WITCH
EYES JUST STARING! STARING STARING
WITCHES IN HER BACKGROUND - THIS MUST ALSO BE BROKEN FOR PEACE IS HAD, THROUGH JESUS
SHAWL
WOMAN UPSET ABOUT MANY THINGS_
OLD WOMAN TRYING TO STARE ME OFF FROM PRAYING WITH THIS PARTICULAR WOMAN.
KEPT SUPER IMPOSING OVER THIS WOMAN

It is very important when deliverance is being done for these evil spirits not to go into another one present that is not spirit-filled. Caution should be taken. If there is nothing for them to enter, they whither. Have no one or even your pet animal present when deliverance is being done. Only through true spirit-filled believers, who are under the blood of Jesus Christ, can there be victory. Be led by the Holy Spirit in these matters, not of self. Use caution and much prayer. This is a delicate mater. Not everyone is led to do this ministry. Wait for much confirmation before attempting this.

Even while attempting to write this particular segment of my book, by the leading of the Holy Spirit, I am experiencing a heavy, oppressive feeling. I am exhausted and feel a loss of energy, but thank God I am under the blood of Jesus Christ. I am thankful that I have the peace of the Lord and His protection. Anyone who is not truly under the blood of Jesus should not attempt to explore any of these areas. It is truly dangerous. Even though being filled with the Holy Spirit, one can still feel the effects of the heavy, oppressive hovering. One must be filled with the Holy Spirit, and wait for much confirmation of His leading, to minister in these areas of deliverance.

It is amazing how these confused human beings, the carnal Christians, will search you out to pray for them when the going gets rough. They automatically know they will get relief by just being in a spirit-filled person's presence. However, the oppressed and nearly possessed person will shy away from the spirit-filled person when the name of Jesus is used. They won't want to be around you. They will feel very uncomfortable. Satan won't let them go. They are in his hands, and it will be a terrible, exhaustive encounter to try to free them. It takes more than one person to do this deliverance, but remember one thing: there is victory in Jesus Christ. Just believe it and come to Him. He will never forsake you, so reach out in time, before death. They, themselves, reach out periodically for spirit-filled people to pray for them.

Unfortunately, many are going for prayer and obtain a temporary healing from the counterfeit. Many are false prophets and are getting their power from the evil one, because they are not under the blood of Jesus and have not accepted Jesus Christ as

106
THAT MAN'S BLACK HUGE SATANIC HUMAN LIKE EVIL SPIRIT
FACE HAZY
WHENEVER ANYONE TALKS TO THIS MAN ABOUT JESUS, THIS HUGE BLACK FIGURE BLOCKS HIM OFF COMPLETELY BY STANDING IN FRONT OF HIM + OVERSHADOWING HIM!
QUICK SKETCH

their Lord and Savior. They do not believe Jesus Christ died for our sins, also, and in essence all this is scripturally stated, as them being the spirit of the antichrist.

As of this moment, the study group has broken up. Some moved on to other avenues of, I don't know where; some totally dedicated their lives to Jesus Christ and are spirit filled. Some are still floundering, searching for the truth, in the darkness. Some are oppressed and some are on the verge of possession.

I could see, at this time, Jesus Christ leading me out of even witnessing any more to these people. I had a terrible burden in the beginning, to bring the scripture reading to them for them to see the light, but they just wouldn't respond and still chose to go their own way. So, I have done my part and, at this time, will continue to just pray for the grace of God to be bestowed upon them so that they can see the light and come into the fullness of where they should be. Satan has them blocked at this time, and surely they need deliverance. Some have no belief in Holy Scripture and no faith. Hopefully, somewhere, Jesus will lead them into a deliverance service. We are still praying for them, unto death do we part. And after that, the judgment!

They were one of the greatest groups, before Satan entered in and started to oppress them. They were a loving group, very interesting, one of the greatest when they were under and asking for the protection of the Archangel Michael and the power of Jesus Christ. Somewhere, someplace, Satan and his demons began to filter in and threw everything off course. These far-out teachings opened the doors for demonic influence when they got off base from the teachings of Jesus himself.

One man in particular, who thought he had it all together, is off going to a woman healer, who rejects even the personality of God and does not believe in the three persons of God. She also believes Jesus was a mere man and his preexistence. She is a well-known psychic and working out of a well-known Christian Church. She is a false prophet, and not of God, using her psychic powers to heal, which may stem from the powers of darkness. So many people are being deceived by her and, unfortunately, she may be the one who will stand before the Lord and say, "Lord, Lord, in they name didn't we prophesy, heal and perform many wonderful miracles?" But He does say, "Depart from me, ye that work iniquity. I never knew you," Matthew 7. This so-called healer is not saved and her power does not come from Jesus Christ, through the Holy Spirit. By rejecting the deity of Jesus Christ and scripture in Deuteronomy 18, her healing does not come from God. 1 John 4:1-3, "Beloved, believe not every spirit, but try the spirits whether they are of God, because many false prophets are gone into the world. Hereby know ye the spirit of God. Every spirit that confesseth that Jesus Christ is come in the flesh is of God; and every spirit that confesseth not that Jesus Christ is come in the flesh is not of God, and this is the spirit of the antichrist, whereof ye have heard that it should come; and even now is already in the world."

At this very moment, I lift this particular person and his sister up to Jesus Christ, for them to recognize the truth and to be saved. This man and his sister are going to this healer every Thursday. I pray they will come to the light where she is concerned, for he will also lead others away from this false healer. Heal? Yes, she does, but who would want to be healed by the powers of darkness. His usual payment is your soul! Depart from him, you that read this while you are still alive. Repent for your sins and involvement with her and be free from the powers of hell. May the power of the Holy Spirit lead you out of the darkness and her oppression.

Jesus came to give life. Accept Him and ask Him to come into your hearts and be healed. The peace of the Lord Jesus Christ will be with you. Be with Him in paradise! Come to Him! He died for yours sins. Accept this wonderful sacrifice and get under the blood of Jesus Christ. Be saved by Jesus Christ and not by this woman, who openly rejects him as Lord and Savior, so therefore is not under the blood of Jesus.

Another couple in the group just seems to be under bondage and unable to move in any direction. My concern led me to a revelation from God that there were witches in their background, and unless this bond with that connection is broken, they will be under bondage. They, themselves, must recognize this and rebuke all witchcraft in their past generations, in the name of Jesus Christ, and get under the blood of Jesus to be free. I pray they will recognize this.

BY SATAN
BOUND!
BOUND!
CONFUSION
WITCHES
WIFE
HUSBAND

The woman is like a sponge; she absorbs so many things. She is bound by fear to enter into many relationships. She must get under the blood and have Jesus take upon himself all that she herself absorbs. Otherwise, exhaustion will overtake her.

The gentleman seems to stay alive by the energy around others, but unless he is around Spirit-filled people, he is taking in evil energy and feeding the demons more and more. They, in turn, are keeping him in bondage. He, too, must get under the blood of Jesus Christ or the demons will devour him. There is so much confusion. This couple is quite unique. At this time in place, the bondage has them so bound that they are out of circulation and isolated.

This couple, too, had witches in their background, and unless this is recognized and rejected in the name of Jesus, there will be a constant spiritual battle going on – to and fro, here nor there, very intense restlessness. Other people involved in witchcraft will be constantly attracted toward them. No peace will prevail. There will be a pull in the right direction and then the evil one will draw them back into his beliefs, back and forth, back and forth. Spells will be on the rampage and constant battle to ward them off. It will be exhausting for both of them. They will stare and stare into oblivion.

Their past generations, who were involved with witches, must be broken! Particularly the male in this episode as he will no longer communicate. His eyes will stare off into the distance and not move at all. He will be found. This man was a great leader, a man witch, casting spells called a quick witch.

Even now, there is another woman witch attracted to him, who keeps coming to their house. It is without a doubt a connection to the attraction. There is danger in this relationship. The air has to be cleared by prayer when she is on the scene. Her specialty is casting spells. If this family is not under the blood of Jesus Christ and His protection, these spells will take place. There is victory in Jesus. Nothing will penetrate if this is so. Nothing will touch the children of God. Praise the Lord.

LEADER
MAN WITCH
QUICK
SKETCH
SPELLS
QUICK
WITCH
A HUGE SATAN
FIGURE IS STARTING
TO TAKE POSSESSION
OF HIM - A HUGE MAN
SITTING IN A HUGE
CHAIR! DATE OF
REVEALATION
4/30/78

Another woman was on her way to glory and coming to the fullness of the Holy Spirit, but became bogged down by other people influencing her. They used the spirit of ridicule when any mention of salvation through Jesus was discussed. There were no so-called spirits hovering around her that I could see with the eyes of the spirit. There were many unhappy times and one great unfortunate happening. It was the loss of her husband, which resulted in widowhood. It was mentioned that perhaps she had involvements in the occult, seances, etc., not realizing the seriousness of these matters. Although I could not see anything with the eyes of the spirit, I can't help but wonder if the spirit of suicide was hovering around, even though I could not see it. This is the subtlest spirit and could mask itself so that it would strike suddenly. Somehow it could not be seen, as though this spirit was invisible. There was also a spirit of confusion there at times. Every so often the air would clear and Jesus was asked to come into her life, however at these times, certain people were ridiculing this whole Jesus scene. She would resort to comments that were not truly biblical, especially on morality.

To be repentant of all things in her past will bring her to accept Jesus Christ as her personal Lord and Savior. She will then be under the blood of Jesus, if she believes that Jesus died for our sins. There will be new life in Christ, and she will begin to recognize the obstacles that are put in her path preventing her from coming to the fullness. Other people's problems at this time are shooting forth, and she is questioning their lives instead of stepping out in faith and giving all of herself to Jesus Christ. The right relations will get her through. I pray that she will recognize this. There is so much fullness ahead for her in regard to relationships, but she clings to old ways that are not really bringing her the joys of this earthly life. Each day could be so rewarding, would be unbelievable, if only she would step out on faith and not worry about those who accepted Christ and then had so many weaknesses and problems only because they did not get into the right fellowship, read God's words and draw on the power. Too many times people are too willing and quick to give into the other power, which will not bring life to that person. The intellectual and the emotional struggle is always hindering with sarcasm. This person was so close, but at such a standstill, for there are so many distractions that are hindering coming to the top.

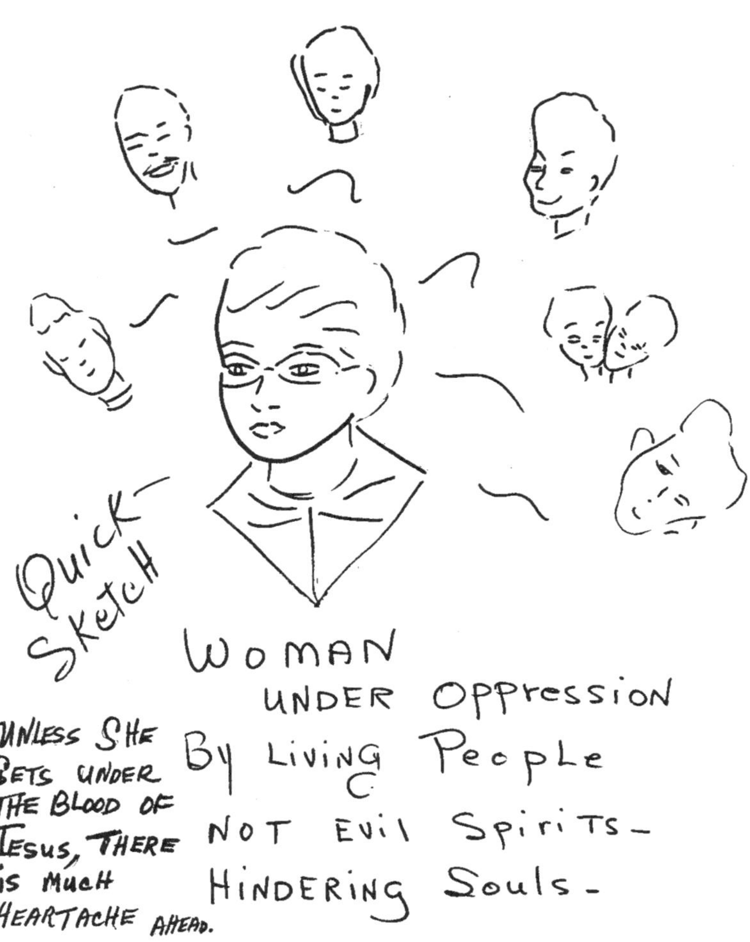

Then there was the vice-principal, a very warm and very fine young man. There were no spirits or hindering people around him that could be seen. The only thing I detected was a black cloud hovering in the background. A dead black man's occult involvements were seeking to influence him. I've lost contact with this young man, however by the leading of the Holy Spirit, we will meet again this Sunday. He must be especially cautious not to be in any contact with this dead black man's spirit, for it will be a demon having him believe it is his friend. He is the one that this demon will have him think that it is through him that this black man wants to make contact. Have nothing to do with it! It will be dangerous and have a very bad influence on him.

I have met him again on Sunday, and I found out that he deals with the discipline of the school children. I hope and pray that he will deal with the spirits of these children who are having these problems. It is in the spiritual realm that one will recognize what is influencing these young boys and girls. Never before are these known influences hovering, because of so many people involved in the occult and drawing these spirits here in the earth plane. It is causing chaos, and no one can quite understand why. We must clear the air through prayer and wiping out the occult involvements. If this is not done, there will be more and more possession taking place, especially among the young and old who are opening themselves by using drugs and so much alcohol. Oppression is around so many, but it will get worse by seeing so many possessed by the evil spirits.

These people must be brought under the blood of Jesus, by accepting Him as their Lord and Savior. Then Jesus will give them the power to be truly sons of God. Mass evangelization must take place.

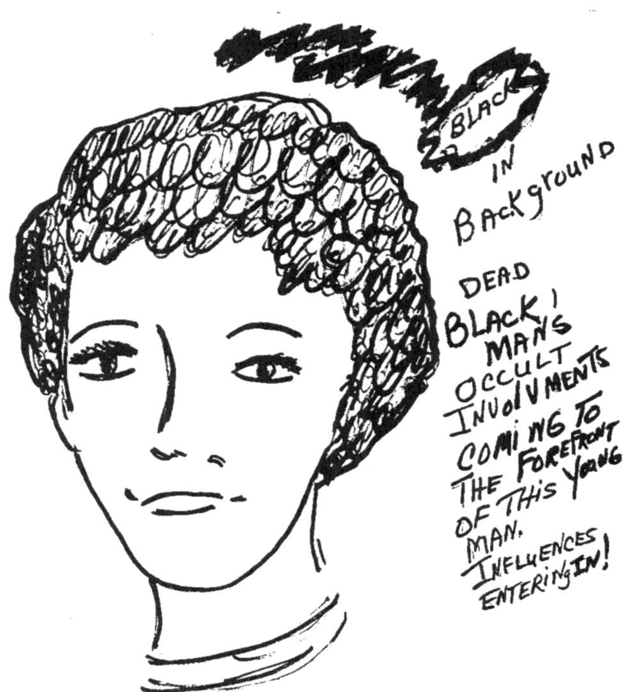

THERE IS A BLOCK – OF SOMEKIND HERE
IN THIS VERY GENTLE MAN.

? ? ? ?

This delightful old woman with her dancing spirit seemed the most difficult. The Holy Spirit revealed as a young child that she was very pampered by her father. Her mother was out of the picture for some reason when this was all revealed. She seemed to feed and be thrilled by this pampering and spent a great deal of time in bed. She was so oppressed and misled, completely blocked, that there seemed no way out for her. She has been the most difficult to capture. The essence of what she is all about is very flighty – here nor there, solid, very airy, so much fantasy and very poetic.

I am led to the scripture of Song of Solomon, chapter 2, as I think of her. "I am the rose of Sharon and the lily of the valleys. As the lily among thorns, so is my love among daughters. As the apple tree among the trees of wood, so is my beloved among the sons. I sat down under his shadow with great delight and his fruit was sweet to my taste. He brought me to the banqueting house, and his banner over me was love." Let he who understands, know what is here at this moment.

I am also led to Psalm 150, "Praise ye the Lord, praise God in his sanctuary. Praise him in the firmament of his power. Praise him for his mighty acts. Praise him according to his excellent greatness. Praise him with the sound of the trumpet. Praise him with the psaltery and harp. Praise him with the timbrel and dance. Praise him with stringed instruments and organs. Praise him upon the loud cymbals. Praise him upon the high sounding cymbals. Let everything that hath breath praise the Lord. Praise ye the Lord."

She is now ailing with cancer. Everything seems hopeless. We now need a miracle. Even though we have been praying for her, it seems that every time she is lifted up for prayer, it is to pray that she will accept Jesus Christ as her Lord and Savior and to stop all of these occult involvements. We pray for her to get under the power of Jesus and to forget all that is misleading her. It is through Jesus that one will get to the Father Almighty. Jesus himself said, "I am the way, the truth and the life. No one comes to the father but through me." It is appointed unto man, once to die and then the judgment. There is no coming back! This is scriptural!

However, at a group prayer time, in the spirit, I was told to pray for a healing for her. I can't imagine this, with the doctor's views on the diagnosis. As time is going on, I will have more to report on this, as the Holy Spirit leads. Time will be of essence to bring her to the light of the true Savior, and not to have her confused with Satan, who also came as an angel of light. I certainly pray that she will recognize the counterfeit. Even the elect will be deceived, so it is written. So many of us have to lift her up in payer.

I was then led by the Holy Spirit to pray for a healing for her on June 28, 1978, at my home church prayer group, who had gathered around the altar.

Time will tell and prove itself by a confirmation. It is too early to tell. I must now make contact with her and tell her of this revelation.

I am trying and struggling to find some sort of community, for it is known that Christians need fellowship to counteract the worldly. Support is needed, especially to study the word of God.

The first study group that really consisted of so-called Christians turned out to have the most beautiful, loving people involved, however it became marbleized with the occult. Perhaps in sincere searching to communicate with God, they did not realize that much bordered on those things forbidden by God, for example, astrology. The so-called fun games, with the crystal ball and cards, were in fun, but certainly they were dabbling in very dangerous territory. Thank God there were no seances or heavy dabblings. While studying the word of God and realizing that all of this is forbidden in His word, I withdrew immediately from the study group. Recognizing that these were not the gifts of the Holy Spirit that I was seeking to learn more about. There was so much good study going on, but it was too bad that these things began to creep in. Reincarnation was another big issue that led me to recognize that this was contrary to God's word. For in God's word, it is written so plainly in Hebrews 9:27, "And it is appointed unto men to die, but after this the judgement." There is no coming back and coming back. God's word is true!

There were so many good studies that were going on, which were in accord with Holy Scripture, that it really was sad that the counterfeit managed to filter in. Many clergy and laity were involved. Seeing the clergy there led me to believe that this was

QUICK SKETCH
THE PAMPERED GIRL
YEARS + YEARS AGO
OLD WOMAN - NOW.

okay. After having such poor teaching on these matters in the mainline church, I was not fully aware of what this scene was all about.

Going on the assumption that these were Christians, I neglected to take the time to investigate where all of this originated, etc. However, knowing many of these people who were leading citizens in the community, everything seemed all right. After being with them so long and getting into this particular study, I thank God for the two young men, John and Mike, and of course there is a third man, Neil, who helped me sort things out very rapidly.

I began to question more and more and with great caution. I questioned the communication or communion of Saints. Were they to mean communication with the dead, which is forbidden by God? They also believed that the miracles of the Bible were the same as the psychic gifts that are on the scene today, E.S.P. etc. I soon came to the understanding that psychic phenomena were not gifts from God, for many of the people involved did not accept Jesus Christ as both divine and human, but repeatedly said that he was a reincarnation of Moses, Buddha, etc. True gifts are of God and were certainly given to born again, spirit-filled Christians. Psychic powers were in the soul force and not in the spirit, where they can always be confused from the standpoint that the devil can enter those thought areas, but cannot filter into the Spirit, for this belongs only to God our Father, through our Lord Jesus Christ. The conscience area can be an easily accessible area to the demonic influences of the devil. So especially when one places one's body in any passive state through meditation, yoga, deep hypnosis, etc., those methods can be dangerous in opening oneself to demonic oppression or even possession. Even those involved with alcohol or drugs to put themselves in a passive state can open up centers for possession by evil spirits.

The truly born again, spirit-filled Christian, who is truly under the blood of Jesus Christ, can only allow himself, through prayer and praise to communicate or commune with God through Jesus. One must be truly under the blood of Jesus to even attempt this, to converse through, talk together, exchange ideas or sentiments and have friendly conversations. 1 Corinthians 2:10-15, "But God hath revealed them unto us by His Spirit; for the Spirit searcheth all things, yea, the deep things of God. For what man knoweth the things of a man, save the spirit of man which is in him? Even so the things of God knoweth no man, but the Spirit of God. Now we have received not the spirit of the world, but the spirit which is of God; that we might know the things that are freely given to us of God. Which things also we speak, not in the words which man's wisdom teacheth, but which the Holy Ghost teacheth; comparing spiritual things with the spiritual. But the natural man recevieth not the things of the spirit of God, for they are foolishness unto him; neither can he know them, because they are spiritually discerned. But he that is spiritual judgeth all things, yet he himself is judged of no man, and also let me add; For who hath known the mind of the Lord, that he may instruct him? But we have the mind of Christ." Read on in that chapter. There is a great message there.

When I became involved in my sincerity, I assumed that these supernatural acts came from God, the healings and tongues. (Come to think of it, I never heard anyone there in that group speak any time in tongues!) After a while I realized these Christians were all mixed in certain beliefs and all that was happening was not of God, but coming under the guise of the counterfeit. Some of these happenings could be from the devil. Plus, reading my Bible, while in my Catholic faith, was not too encouraged as we do today. I, too, came to realize that scripture told us all the false prophets that were going out into the world. Especially by hearing in conversations, most of these people believed that Jesus was a mere man, etc. This turned me off completely. Perhaps the turning point of having me leave the group, in spite of my love for all of them, was when I read 1 John 4:1-6, "Beloved, believe not every spirit, but try the spirits whether they are of God; because many false prophets gone out into the world. Hereby know ye the Spirit of God: Every Spirit that confesseth that Jesus Christ is come in the flesh is of God; and every spirit that confesseth not that Jesus Christ is come in the flesh is not of God and that this the spirit of antichrist, whereof ye have heard that it should come; and even now is it in the world. Ye are of God, little children, and have overcome them; because greater is he that is in you, than he is in the world. They are of the world; therefore speak they of the world, and the world hearth them. We are of God; he that knoweth God heareth us; he that is not of God heareth not us. Hereby know the spirit of truth, and the spirit of error.

So many of the so-called Christians in there believed that you had to work out your own salvation by spiritual progression in this life and the next lifetime after being reincarnated. This is not in agreement with the Bible. If man could save himself, then Christ's death on the cross was not necessary. Jesus is the only means to salvation, as it was written. They take only what is written to suit themselves, and flatly contradict the Bible and say it was for those times. How deceived they are!

It is very hard for them to accept the idea that God would send people to Hell. Spirit goes back to God, but the soul goes to a place of judgment, heaven or hell, as it is written. The choice is all yours. Jesus spoke about hell many times in scripture. It is your choice to either accept Jesus Christ as your Lord and Savior. It is yourself that sends your soul to one place or the other. It is as simple as that. I must stress this point that it is not one to get caught up in a great deal of emotionalism, and not be in the true spirit of the Holy Spirit. However, emotions do play a part in the total commitment. God wants all of you, including your emotions. But of course it goes much deeper to not only include head knowledge and historical knowledge, but heart totally. The true bride of Christ must give her heart. Revelations 22:17, "And the Spirit and the bride say, Come. And let him that heareth say, Come. And let him that is arthritic come. And whosoever will, let him take the water of life freely."

Just recently there was a gathering of several of the study group, because there seemed to be death in sight for a few. One is dying of cancer. The other one seems lost. It is revealed that the one who is lost will go first. There just seems to be a block where this brother and sister are involved. There is a healer woman who has them in bondage, leading them astray. Jesus Christ is the healer, all glory and honor is his, not hers! A deliverance service must be held somewhere to draw them out of her hands. This is my prayer. A cancerous death is also hovering, and much confusion is setting in. I am waiting for the leading of the Holy Spirit where they are concerned. There just seems to be a block! There is much prayer needed for more revelation as to what we can do to help bring them to salvation.

The other older woman dying of cancer is still a beautiful woman with such a dancing spirit. The Lord has revealed to me that she will be reached for the Lord, through dance and poetry. We must also put her in intense light! There is much prayer and work to have a miracle.

Before the end comes for these older people, I will just have more to report before this book is completed. I am waiting for a leading and direction in this matter.

WE MUST GET THEM OUT OF THE CONFUSION THIS WOMAN IS BRINGING THEM—JESUS IS LORD NOT HER! THE SO CALLED HEALER—JESUS IS THE HEALER, ALL GLORY IS HIS, NOT HERS.

A BEAUTIFUL WOMAN—LEANS TOWARD WOMEN - DANCING SPIRIT—REACHED THROUGH DANCE + POETRY. TOO MANY DIRECTIONS—JESUS IS THE WAY BLINDNESS MUST BE TAKEN AWAY BY INTENSE LIGHT

Chapter 10
The Charismatic Church Prayer Group

I was led to go back to this particular meeting, still searching over for my group. I knew that to be in the world and yet not of the world, I needed that spiritual fellowship and prayerful atmosphere. Still not really knowing that it was here that God wanted me, I decided to give it a part of my time. However, it soon became known that it was not here that the Lord wanted me, although the people involved were very loving people and it was wonderful to be with them. They loved the Lord Jesus Christ very, very much and surely wanted themselves under his Lordship, as I did. However, there was an undertone of something not right. I did not quite understand it as yet. Time and time again I prayed about attending the prayer meetings, and I did go several times, but each time I felt that the Lord didn't want me there, for He had other plans for me, especially in devoting my extra time in writing this book. Plus, He kept leading me into more fellowship with the youth, especially the college-aged young men and women, even older ones already out of college. He was gently leading me into the music area. The ministry of music???

The concerts where Jesus music was performed showed me exactly where our youth were and the type of music that this particular group liked. The love just flowed in the name of Jesus Christ at those concerts. The beauty of it was that all ages were present and really enjoying it very much. They were really being ministered to. There was no age barrier; they just loved one another. It was just beautiful. Their music was beginning to be a great ministry in the body of Christ and was leading so many others to commit their lives to Jesus and to be obedient to His word. Their music was reaching people like preaching never could. They were enjoying so much together, playing Bible games and having so much fun. It really brought joy into their lives. I could see many who were floundering getting their lives together and becoming serious as to what they thought God wanted of them. Their total dedication was just great, however they had to practice patience, for the Lord was not revealing Himself as readily as they thought He should. We all knew He was working something in their lives, for we could see the change taking place in their lives. It was beautiful!

Getting back to the Charismatic Group... I seem to go from one thing to another, but that is how my life is going. There is so much happening all the time. But for the group at the church, I am still searching to see if God wants me to continue there. The past two weeks, I have not been led there. Although they are a fine group, I feel that God wants me elsewhere. I must be obedient to His will.

There are so many doors opening and I must pray to see where I must give my total dedication, after this book is written. The Christian Supper Clubs are on the scene here again. There will be Christian entertainment and music, which again is the great way to minister to the body of Christ. Plus Christians should be having fun and enjoying life in all its fullness. There is such a need in this area. Our Christian young men and women have devoted so much time and energy in studying their music with nowhere to play and share it. This would be just wonderful. I do feel led to see what this is all about. As usual, there are so many doors opening. I pray for God to lead to the priorities of where He would want me. There are so many good causes and groups, however, I know the only way they will be fruitful is for Him to be in charge and lead the way. I seem to be leaning in that direction, involved in a music ministry that is, and not necessarily playing music, but something to do in that area. Time and prayer will tell. I've been to and have seen so many weak music ministries, which are a vital part of praising and worshiping God.

My past experience of going to this Charismatic Prayer Group on several occasions led me to a special girl. I believe that the Holy Spirit led us together on one occasion. The first time she entered the church of the prayer group, I was present and noticed her crying in the church pew. I was led to talk to her and told her

I would pray with her. We talked about many things without delving into anything specific. What was especially drawn from the conversation was that she had not fully accepted Jesus Christ as her Lord and Savior, even though she was a Catholic and in the church. I immediately recognized this and told her that no matter what, there is only life in Jesus. I told her that she must step out on faith and accept Jesus and that He died for our sins. She said she knew that, but couldn't do it. I realized that she was under oppression. I told her I would continue to pray for her and her family. I hadn't seen her for a while and didn't go every week to the prayer group.

One week, as I was led there and as the prayer group gathered, she came in and sat for a while with the group. All of a sudden, she started to cry and went off the side altar, up the aisle, through the door, and outside she went. At first I felt led to go after her, but then decided not to, but to go into prayer immediately for her. I asked the Lord to watch over and protect her. There at the Charismatic Prayer Group, there were things being said and revealed that were causing the spirit within me to cry out with love and concern for a few there present. There were undertones of such bondage. Christ came to give us life abundantly, not sadness and bondage, which seemed to permeate. Sacrifice was still given by some and Jesus didn't want that. He was the ultimate sacrifice! He came to show us the way and to give us life in all its fullness. We should be there to receives this. Vows of poverty, chastity and obedience were not what he was seeking. Obedience, yes, to His word, but not poverty and chastity as they saw it. Life should be lived in its divine fullness, according to His word.

My spirit seemed to want to cry out to a nun present, but I decided not to cause any waves, so to speak. There was needed here the trust in the leading of the Holy Spirit, for there was so much leading done by oneself and the self planning. The self was still controlling there. In this group, there was a dire need of stepping out on faith, to allow the Holy Spirit to minister. It was very puzzling at times at the certain lack of genuine love. This kind of love was coming from several present there. It really was not genuine love. There, too, was coldness...demonstrative actions...but no depth of love. It was very superficial. Then again, with some others there was this genuine warmth and love. As much as I am looking and searching for a true, spirit-filled fellowship, I don't think I will find it with this particular group, although there are several whom I love very dearly and can relate to well.

The crying girl came to visit me at work. I was so happy to see her. She explained that she was always looking for me at the payer meetings, but saw that I was not coming. She related that the last time I was there, she was so engrossed with a newborn baby, which seemed to get to her that she just had to leave. Plus all that was happening in her life, she began crying and left quickly.

There is a leading of the Holy Spirit here, between us two, and I must be spiritually aware of all that is taking place. She entered the room here, and I am seeing with the eyes of the spirit an influence over her, which is demonic in nature. She, herself, is a very good, warm, loving, sincere person. This demonic hovering is getting ready to challenge me fiercely. I must be led by the Holy Spirit in dealing in specifics.

From the conversation with her, there was a monk who prayed over her, and this monk killed his wife, etc. The rest of what she said I did not retain, but that I did. I now questioned if this monk was truly under the blood of Jesus Christ when he prayed over her. Plus, if she had not fully accepted Jesus Christ as her Lord and Savior, this could be a dangerous area. One must be spirit-filled to do this, that is, the laying on of hands and praying over anyone. These are delicate areas. I know Satan knows all of the knowledge that I now have in regard to all of his and that I can also lead and direct her. This demonic hovering is trying to frighten me off. Satan is saying to me, "I'll have the other members of the prayer group think that it was because you were there that she walked out of the prayer meeting." I know that Jesus Christ is going to have victory here, for we will continue to pray for her and her family, for I am aware of His leading us together. Satan is placing all kinds of obstacles in the way of seeing or coming into contact with this crying girl, but we will make contact gain. And she will be ministered to in the name of Jesus.

Already I can see the demonic hovering. Satan is getting all confused and doesn't now what to do for his next attack. With our authority over this, I'm sure he will flee. We must weed all the garbage this girl has very much collected throughout her past involvements.

There is so much going on in so many directions at this time. I must go into a quiet time to listen and follow the leading of the Holy Spirit.

There are always supernatural happenings that take place, if one is spiritually aware, especially when you are in a prayer group and in a state of grace.

This vision occurred one morning while in prayer near the church altar. The crucifix was on the altar and all of a sudden, this seemed to be superimposed over it. The Lord is revealing to me that once the world would get under the Lordship of Jesus Christ, there would be so many blessings poured out. And unbelievable, wonderful visions into the spiritual realm would also be revealed to those in a state of grace. If only people would realize this and get everything into perspective, it would be beyond one's fondest dreams. However, so many with their unbelief are bogging down everything that should be, by throwing obstacles in every direction. Even their thoughts are blocking many of the joys that are to be had. This leads to the direction and understanding of the Rapture and God taking us out of this world. Jesus is coming soon. Prepare ye the way for the Lord! Repent for your sins, accept Jesus Christ as your Lord and Savior, get under the blood of Jesus, believe that He died for your sins, step out on faith, for it is through faith, by grace, that we are saved. Praise God!

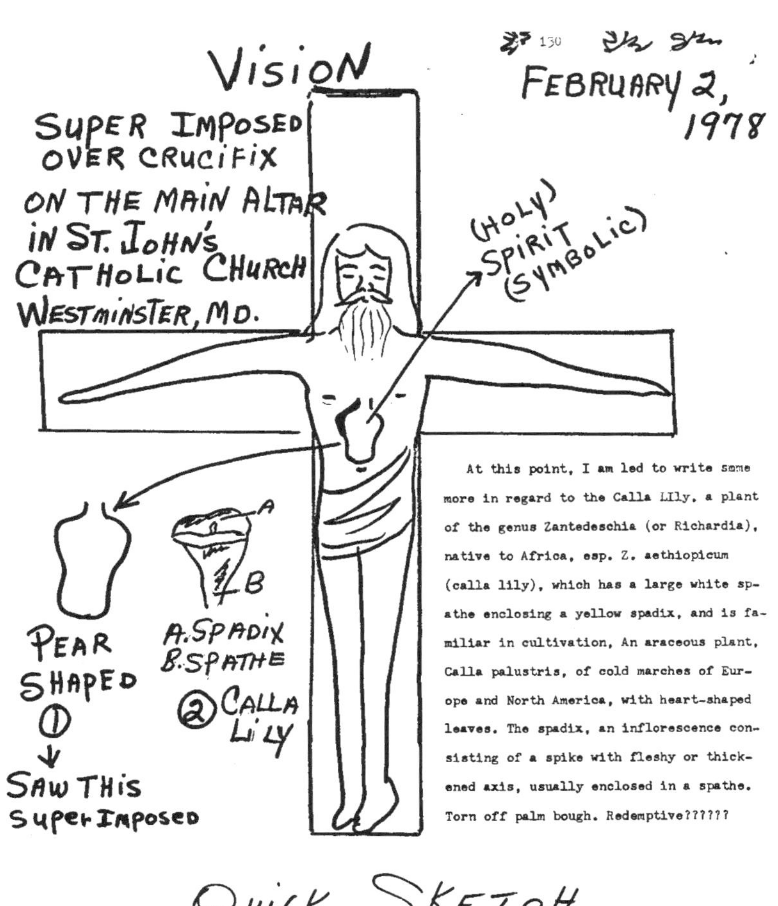

At this point, I am led to write same more in regard to the Calla LIly, a plant of the genus Zantedeschia (or Richardia), native to Africa, esp. Z. aethiopicum (calla lily), which has a large white spathe enclosing a yellow spadix, and is familiar in cultivation, An araceous plant, Calla palustris, of cold marches of Europe and North America, with heart-shaped leaves. The spadix, an inflorescence consisting of a spike with fleshy or thickened axis, usually enclosed in a spathe. Torn off palm bough. Redemptive??????

Chapter 11
The Evening Church Prayer Group

It seems in the very beginning, before the Charismatic Morning Group formed, I was being led to reenter an evening prayer group. Finally after being in prayer about this, it was listed in the bulletin that there would be an evening group forming. I attended, almost hesitating, for I had been disappointed in the many others that I tried to have fellowship in. However, after praying about this, I decided to give it a try, and if the Holy Spirit did not want me here, I soon would be told.

There had been several people attending, but then the group seemed to dwindle down to a working nucleus, those of whom had a great discussion period. At certain times, one is always concerned with numbers, but by the leading of the Holy Spirit, this does not seem too important at this point. We are praying for the leading and direction of the Holy Spirit and the support of the church in this area. So many of our people have stopped at salvation, but hesitate to press on for the second experience, the baptism of the Holy Spirit and the exercising and manifestation of the Gifts of the Holy Spirit. The spirit of fear has to be exorcised from the church and brought to the fullness of His glory! Then, too, those other people who are in the church, as well as the so-called Christians who have not truly accepted Jesus Christ as their personal Lord and Savior, have to be prayed with to at least get them salvation. No one should take for granted that people who are going through all the motions of being Catholic, Christian, or whatever denomination have salvation when they truly do not. This is doing them an injustice, for God searches the hearts of men. Not all of them there have truly accepted Jesus as the only way to the Father. Perhaps in ministering to these certain few that think all religions are okay, should read the Salvation scriptures.

All these false gods, or Eastern philosophies, or whatever else, are not the way to the Father. The salvation scriptures are as follows:

John 14:6, Jesus said, "I am the way, the truth and the life; no man can come to the Father except by me." John 3:18, "He that believes in me is not condemned, but he that does not believe is condemned already because he has not believed in the name of the only begotten Son of God." John 8:23,224, "Ye are from beneath; I am from above; ye are of this world. I am not of this world. I said therefore unto you, that ye shall die in your sins; for if ye believe not that I am he, ye shall die in your sins." Acts 4:12, "Neither is there salvation in any other." Proverbs 14:12, "There is a way which seemeth right unto man; but the end thereof are the ways of death."

It is my prayer that all comes to Salvation. One would have to step out in faith, which is the substance of things hoped for, the evidence of things not seen, that is found in Hebrews 11:1. "For it is through faith by grace that we are saved!" Of course graces comes through the Holy Spirit. It is written also in the Acts of the Apostles 1:5, "For then John truly baptized with water; but ye shall be baptized with the Holy Ghost not many days hence." Acts 1:7,8, "And he said unto them 'It is not for you to know the times or the seasons, which the Father hath put in his own power. But ye shall receive power after that the Holy Ghost is come upon you; and ye shall be witnesses unto me both in Jerusalem and in all Judea, and in Samaria, and unto the outermost part of the earth.'" John 14:26, "But the Comforter, which is the Holy Ghost, whom the Father will send in my name, he shall teach you all things and bring all things to your remembrance, whatsoever I have said unto you." John 16:7-15, "Nevertheless I tell you the truth; it is expedient for you that I go away, for if I go not away, the Comforter will not come unto you; but if I depart, I will send him unto you. And when he is come, he will reprove the world of sin and of righteousness and of judgment; of sin, because they believe not on me; of righteousness because I go to my Father and ye see me no more; of judgment, because the prince of this world is judged. I have yet so many things to say unto you, but ye cannot hear them now. Howbeit when he, the Spirit of truth is come, he will guide you into all truth, for he shall not speak of himself, but whosoever he shall hear, that shall he speak; and he will show you things to come. He shall glorify me, for he shall receive of mine and shall show it unite you. All things that the Father hath are mine: therefore said I, that he shall take of mine and shall show it unto you." Praise God! Christ comforts his disciples.

Prayer takes us into a great, mysterious, beautiful, spiritual realm, giving us a clear view. It is awesome at times and we must use wisdom in capturing the view and relating it through mere words. Things begin to happen when a prayer group begins to pray, especially when there is harmony, peace and fellowship among the believers. Acts 4:32, "And the multitude of them that believed were of one heart and of one soul." After this it is written, "And with great power," etc., for it never fails that when God's people are of one heart and one soul, that great power and grace will rest upon them. It is extremely important for all to be in unity, that is all Christians everywhere, for this God power to truly work. We are to see miracles beyond belief once this takes place. It is time for the body of Christ to stop tearing Christ's body apart. It is now the time to get this unity through Jesus Christ and allow the power to manifest itself!

It also never fails that once a prayer group begins to form, there are all kinds of demonic effects trying to scatter it. Satan hates to see a prayer group forming, for he does know the power of prayer. No matter what there is on the scene, the group must hold fast and be overcomers. Then watch and see the power work!

As we function as a prayer group, even then we must have a very close walk with Jesus, for through the Holy Spirit, he will lead us as to how and what to pray for in certain circumstances. It is not just to pray for all healings; sometimes it is better to pray that the Father will take them to heaven to be with Him. It is extremely important, when one is asked to pray for someone, to immediately lift that person up to Jesus and ask for the leading of the Holy Spirit as to what He would have us do. For example, there was a 71 year old woman who was in critical condition, and someone called me up to pray for her, that she did not want to live, etc. I listened and immediately asked the Holy Spirit what He would have me do. There was peace felt that we should let her go to the Father. We did lift her up in prayer, but the main concern was that she had salvation and did accept Jesus Christ as her Lord and Savior, "for no man comes to the Father but through me." These were the words of Jesus himself. Even though people are in the church, we must still be certain that they have truly accepted that Jesus died for their sins.

Even in times of being asked for payer, we must always pray for a happy and peaceful death, no matter what. One does not have to go to the father in pain and suffering. More importantly, we must always pray for salvation. If you are walking very close to our Lord, you will know what and how to pray. Also sometimes, you will be led to pray for healing, but many times we hold on to people through prayer when it would be best to allow them to go to the Father.

It is very early to write much on this prayer group. There seems to be differences of opinions, but we are not seeking our opinions but those of the Holy Spirit. I know He will lead as He listens to the sincerity of our hearts. There seems to be a pure love flowing, a little caution, which is good, but one can truly feel the love present, the divine love.

For his people are around, it is just a matter of getting them all together. As the spirit leads, we will follow in obedience. It seems now at this time that everything that is happening is not quite fully understood, but I'm sure as we see the plan of God unfold, we will understand it more. We must step out on faith and allow the Spirit to work His way, not ours. We must constantly put everything in his hands and allow him to use us in the way He knows things should be exercised. We must constantly pray for wisdom, knowledge too, but the wisdom to exercise this knowledge.

There were a larger number of people coming, but many dropped off. For what reasons, we do not quite know. It is now being revealed to me that we should have a special meeting to discuss just exactly what these people expect from a prayer meeting, etc. At the moment, I sense the spirit of fear and puzzlement present. Perhaps, there are those who have come for ordinary prayer, who have stopped at salvation, and those who have been baptized in the Holy Spirit and allowed the gifts to operate in their lives. If one is not baptized by the Holy Spirit, it is very difficult to understand what is going on. One can be bound by fear and rendered at a loss as to what to do or say, as well as be perplexed and bogged down by a connotation of mysteriousness.

It seems that what has been revealed to me, in regard to the spirit of fear, has been confirmed by two other people soon after: a speaker at the Full Gospel Businessmen's Fellowship and a priest. It is really wonderful and inspiring to see how the spirit works among the body of Christ. The scripture reading of Christ speaking about unity among believers was also confirmed Praise the Lord!

It is early to draw any conclusions or evaluations in regard to this evening church prayer group. As time goes on, we shall see what the Holy Spirit has for us.

Chapter 12
A Dream: The light of Christ under His Protection in Hell

In the dream, I was walking through hell, where there were many demons, all kinds, and I was being shown this, that this is truth! I was given a view of this and knew that there was truly a hell... I saw it!

Fortunately, my light, by having Christ within me and under the protection of the blood of Jesus, was too much for them. The demons shielded their faces from me. They didn't want to look at me. I was blinding them; the holiness was too much to bear. It was awful for them! They wanted me to leave. They spent all of their time trying to shield themselves from the light.

I truly was given the great realization that I was a child of God and truly was under His protection. I could walk in victory anywhere.

Periodically I was given this vision of being protected from the evil one. It was only then that I knew I could go into enemy territory and try to rescue the lost sheep. Gradually as time wen on, I can see the plan of God unfolding. Many of the times, while being in enemy territory and bringing the gospel of Christ, there were many led out of evil situations and out of those activities that were occult in nature. These cults are everywhere, even in the small towns where one would think that everything is under control The Lord is revealing to me some very prominent individuals are very much involved in occult matters and are attracting and drawing heavy spiritual warfare in our community. There is no peace in our town; so many young people are in turmoil, using drugs, alcohol, etc. If only they would step out in faith, repent of their sins and accept Jesus Christ as their Lord and Savior and be baptized. It is only by faith through grace that we are saved. We must get under the blood of Jesus Christ and live according to His word, the full gospel.

Oppressive Forces

Oppressive forces are flowing in, as I am proofreading this, forces telling me that I am crazy spending time on this book. I'll never finish and get this all together. There are a great deal of hindering spirits.

As I am trying to proofread, there are so many distractions. A salesman is here on this particular day, plus the bathroom commode has backed up and overflowed; the two simultaneously occurred. Everything is happening to make me say, "Oh, heck with it all." But there is something greater than me that is giving me the inspiration and strength to overcome all of this. Praise God!

The next day, while trying to proofread some of this, I am experiencing much oppression. There are attacks on the physical body trying to stop me. Other upsets, such as the clothes dryer going out of commission, take up more of my time so I would be unable to have more time for my book. The dryer was just burning; the fan broke. One could say this could all happen to anyone at any time, but there is an air of something different hovering that one can detect in the spirit, that this is an attack of the evil one and nothing else. When you live a life in the spirit, you can discern these things. The evil one is out to try to prevent this book from getting into print. This is a book that is going in all directions at once, because so much is happening all at one time in all directions, but there is uniformity and much deep spiritual knowledge and wisdom here, and the evil forces know this. Just when a great blessing is about to take place, the evil forces try to crush your spirit with all kinds of remarks of putting you down, but thank God we are overcomers and recognize this. We won't let them feed on this by talking on and on about the unkind remarks.

Soon after all of this oppressive hovering, my taking authority over all that was happening and not getting discouraged, I was shown what would really be happening if the people would truly get under the blood of Jesus Christ and accept Him as their Lord and Savior and live according to His word. There would be miracles happening beyond belief, healings, etc. For example, I was shown this in another dream, the Blessings Pouring Forth.

The Struggle

In the dream, I saw a young boy standing on a sort of loading dock. He came to the edge and fell forward. It was a high loading dock, and he fell face down, a very hard and solid fall. I then saw that he got up without a scratch. Ordinarily, his face would have been smashed because of the way he fell. The Holy Spirit seemed to commune with me and say, "See the power of the Holy Spirit. You will see many miracles such as this when you are around, and through prayer, you will have this power. Just have this close walk with Lord Jesus Christ."

Then a day or so later, again I was shown in a dream the power of prayer and the gifts in operation to use the knowledge and the wisdom through the leading of the Holy Spirit.

In the dream, I saw another young boy lying on the ground. Someone said, "He is dead." I looked at him and quickly said, "Everybody lay hands on him!" We all did, and then the boy got up and was alive and well! The Holy Spirit said, "There are many miracles ahead for those who believe in me and keep my word. Be ready to use the knowledge and the wisdom that I have given to you." So fellow brothers and sisters in Christ, be ready!

There is also the age of wrath that is coming on the scene for those who do not accept Jesus Christ as their Lord and Savior, but I do not want to dwell on that, for I will soon feel the effects, by being very sensitive.

The Vision of the Earth in Space

As I looked at the photo of the earth in space, I began to see with the eyes of the spirit, these little forming pictures scattered about.

It seemed as a communication took place, the words came forth: "The earth is ready for Birth."

EARTH READY FOR BIRTH
PURE TOP
WHITE
OBSERVATORY
TOWER
RAM
POODLE
DOG
DEVIL!
BLACK
BLACK
LIGHT
WICKED
MAN
flesh
CHILD
FLESH
RAYS O
PROTECTING
CHILD
CRYSALYS
ANGEL WHITE
SCALEY BLACK
ANIMAL
WHITE
Earth
World
FREKISH
FACE

The Evaluation of the Chapters

It is interesting the way in which I am led to list the chapters and to see how they line up with the essence or gist of the value of numbers, in the way they were written.

Chapter 1: The number 1 in the Bible stands for unity. In the meaning here is harmony, peace and fellowship. In Acts 4:32, "And the multitude of them that believed were of one heart and one soul." It never fails when God's people are of one heart and one soul that great power and grace will rest upon them. Jesus prayed for the unity of his believers.

Chapter 2: The Bible number is for division or separation. In Genesis 1:4, "And God divided the light from the darkness." In Kings 3:16-27, two women claiming ownership of two children; one dead and the other alive. They both claimed the living child, etc.

Chapter 3 is associated with Resurrection.

Chapter 4 is associated with the first creation and the flesh. All flesh is not the same – men, beasts, fishes, and birds. The word "creature" is found four times in the account of creation.

Chapter 5 refers to Grace.

Chapter 6: The number 6 is connected to Satan. The sixth commandment is "Thou shall not kill." The number 666, in the Bible, refers to the mark of the beast.

Chapter 7 is connected with completeness, perfection, or bringing to an end.

The fun of these numbers that is very interesting is to find their association in the Bible.

Chapter 8 refers, in number, to the new birth.

And as it is written, so many things and events are happening all at the same time, in all directions, but through it all we have the order and victory in Jesus Christ. So many other new events are taking place, for as I have said, "Everyday is an adventure when leading a life in the spirit." Praise the Lord. He lives!

Chapter 9 refers, in number, to the fruits of the spirit.

Chapter 10, in number, refers to law. The Ten Commandments are laws. Then, God sent his son to redeem those under the law to become sons of God.

Chapter 11 refers to judgment.

Chapter 12 refers, in number, to divine power, authority or rule. Rule of the 12 apostles.

Chapter 13
The Struggle to Get the Book Published

It was around Christmas holiday, and being in retail, we were very busy. It was very enjoyable, but I was tired and needed a break. The plane trip to Texas was great, but things began to get my heart into a tightness which I could not explain. I thought, "Oh well, with the plane ride and being tired out after the holidays, it's only natural." I dismissed all that was taking place. The tightness would be there and then subside. However, in the early morning hours, I woke up with a tightness that would not let up. I then knew that I had better go to the emergency room at the hospital. The doctor there believed I was having a heart attack. The cardiologist entered and explained I would get a T.P.A., but it had to be administered within a certain time. The doctor said that there were risks involved, like I could bleed to death. I then asked what would happen if I would wait and have conventional treatment. He said I could have some heart damage. So I decided to take the T.P.A. I then asked the doctor how soon would I bleed to death if that were the case. He said within 24 hours. Well, everything went well and here I am. Praise God for the victory. I then had more tests and was released from the hospital. I went back to Maryland. There was a huge snowstorm in Maryland, and flights were postponed for a time. We finally were cleared and made it back home. I was so thankful for our neighbor boys who cleared the snow from the driveway, etc., what great men.

I recuperated slowly and finally decided to once again try to get my book published.

That devil was still blocking it and attacking me at every turn of the way.

It was my daughter's birthday and the men would stay at the store business so she and I could go to her favorite Chinese restaurant for dinner. I was driving and all of a sudden I blacked out, hit a tree, and demolished my car. I could hear Jessica call out to me, "Mom!" I started to wake up and something in my spirit said, "Turn your wheel to the right." I did so and I landed in a field. Had I not felt that divine leading, I could have gone into traffic and hit someone. Thank God it was just our car that was demolished. As we landed after flying through the air, my windshield shattered and I looked over at Jessica and asked, "Are you okay?" She said, "Yes, I remembered what position I should take if a plane crashed, and it worked. I'm okay, but shaking like a leaf."

As soon as we crash-landed, a woman opened my car door and asked if we were okay. I said, "Yes," and behind her was a police officer. He told us to get out of the car in case it would explode. He then asked us if we were religious. I answered, "Yes, I'm a believer in Jesus Christ." He said, "You and your daughter should go light a candle, because in accidents like this, the people are dead." God watched over us even when the devil tried to do away with us once again. He doesn't want this book to be published because it gives glory to God. The devil was at work again as I tried to get my energy up to get my book published.

Once Again a Setback

My family and I went shopping one Sunday afternoon. My daughter was asleep in the car, and my husband and I went to the store. While walking back to my car, someone came from behind like a vulture, pulled my purse from my hands and ran to another car waiting for her. I called out to my husband. "She stole my purse!" He ran after her and put his hands on the hood of the car, but had he not moved out of the way, the boy driving the waiting car would have run him over. I called out, "Get their license number!" He said, "They don't have a license plate." And off they drove. We ran back to our car and decided to try and track them. We called to God, "Please help us, Jesus, we need you."

We had no cell phone and didn't want to lose track of them. Before we got to our car, they were nowhere in sight. We drove out of the shopping center and came to a "T" in the road. We didn't know whether to go left or right. Something in my spirit led me to go right. Divine guidance shows itself again. We drove down the road bout a mile and saw a police car on the side of the road with his flashers on. I said to my husband, "Let's go and tell him what happened." As we approached the police car, we saw he had the car and people who stole my purse. We quickly ran to the police officer to tell him that this girl stole my purse. She denied it, and I asked the boy if she had my green purse. He sat there and said, "She doesn't do things like that." I then told the police officer that he would find my purse in their car. He looked under the seat and pulled out my green purse with my identification, etc. I then realized that God did help us. The police officer had a backup car come and he then looked in her purse and saw that she had a needle and drugs. They booked them.

I then asked the police officer why he pulled them over. He said that he was sitting by the bowling alley, watching for people without their seat belts on, and these people were the first to come along. He noticed that they did not have any license tags.

The boy's sister had gotten a new car and took this one off the road. The brother then helped himself to the car without the sister knowing. Thank God that they were caught. Praise God for everything, especially the police officer.

Well, another setback for me to concentrate on my book. Had to go to court as a witness, etc. The struggle continues. She also robbed me of my energy.

Struck and Rear-Ended by Another Driver Who Wanted to Beat the Red Light

My daughter and I went shopping one night. It was raining and we came to a very busy intersection. We stopped for the red light and were rear-ended by another driver who wanted to beat the light. The car jerked us, and we were thrown against the door, after getting whiplash. Thank God I had my seat belt on. I managed to get out of the car to see if there was any damage to my car. The driver never got out of the car to see if we were hurt. He just backed off and sat there. I motioned for him to get out and see what he had done. The car was all scuffed with black, and with the light of the day I could see the paint was all pitted.

I went to a reliable car repair service and got an estimate the next day. I decided not to go to the hospital for a checkup because I knew I had no broken bones. My daughter and I were shook up, for it was frightening experience. Had there not been a leeway on the road, we would have been pushed into oncoming traffic.

The next morning I had muscular aches and pains. My neck and back hurt from the impact. My daughter ached too. I didn't want to make a big deal out of it all. I thought I'd give it a few weeks and it would all go away. Well, after a few weeks, I still didn't feel good, but knew I had an upcoming appointment with my doctor to check me out. When I had my appointment, she found my heart was in arterial fibrillation and said I would have to go to the emergency room. I went right over and they started to treat me. They put me on medication.

The second day, I was feeling terrible. My heart stopped and I passed out. Code Blue was called into my room. The next thing I could hear was them calling my name, "Marie, you passed out and we are trying to revive you." They gave me oxygen, etc. I then asked, "Am I going to make it?" She answered, "We are trying." They also gave me a cardiversion, but it didn't work. They finally got me out of it all, and I was good for another day. Then I began to feel all perspiring and weak. They then called for another cardiversion. That, too, was unsuccessful. They continued medication for a few more days then released me from the hospital. I was to go home for a few days and then reenter another hospital for another cardiversion. That doctor said, "I will do it, for there are tricks to the trade." It was done again and this time it was successful, along with the continued medication. After my heart problems were taken care of, I had to concentrate on my whiplash from the car accident. I then went to a doctor who took X-rays and said I would have to go for physical therapy for my muscle aches and pains. The physical therapy helped, but I must always do my exercises to keep limber. The doctor said it takes months for the body to come to itself after an accident such as this.

As time went on, again my heart went into arterial fibrillation, and I had to go to the hospital and have another cardiversion, which was not successful. The doctor then said he could not

The Car Accident

cardivert me anymore because I already had several. I would have to stay on blood thinners for the rest of my life in order to prevent blood clots and a stroke. My heart was still in arterial fib. The ide effects from all my medication was something I would have live with and tolerate. It was not easy, but it kept me going.

All these setbacks put me behind in getting my book published. I am an overcomer and I will get it done, however, the struggle nues.

am now searching for it to be published. A literary agent ntacted me said friends in the publishing business know I nanuscript to be published. In my search, I find that his name and company is not recommended on the computer. Several subsidy publishers have accepted my manuscript, but I am not led that way. I keep searching to be led by God as to how and where I will be published. It is difficult for an unknown author to be published with an advance from a well-known publisher. I'm like a voice in the wilderness, trying to be heard. I have a great story to tell. God is the author; I am the vehicle.

As time went on, I decided again to pursue publishing my book. We took a vacation to Savannah, Georgia. One the way back home, I began to lose my appetite and was a little sick with a slight fever. We got home. I called my doctor, and she immediately put me in the hospital. Tests proved that I had to have my gallbladder removed. Went through all of that with a breeze, and here I am moving on again to let the world know what a great God we have.

My biggest blocker is always present. I know that the devil works through him at times, to torment me. I had this dream where I was riding in a car with him, and all of a sudden he grabbed me and came after me with a syringe filled with poison. He injected it into my mouth. I said upon waking, "You will not kill me because I did not swallow it." I then spit it out. Strange as it may seem, I did wake up with so much liquid in my mouth. I was confident that God was protecting me. He gave me this book to write and would lead me on. I even wrote a poem entitled "Lead Me On".

The Tests

There are tests that a person will go through in a troubli modern world. One will reach out for divine guidance as to to provide comfort and create some order during this tim

If one decides to go for counseling, remember that th counselor, who determines by the grace of God to k the scripture in his counseling, is the only one wh a solid basis for what he says and does.

It is possible to combine psychological and techniques with Biblical counseling a deeper spiritual walk, whereby prob overcome.

Biblical counseling depends fully on God and is based
principles of scripture. Biblical counseling is love in relati
and truth, because the Lord is the counselor, and because
on the word of God and the Holy Spirit to convict sin ar
obedience.

The apostle Paul warned the Colossians about follc
ways of men. As you receive Christ, so walk in Him, an
been firmly rooted and now being built up in Him and est
in your faith, see to it that no one takes you captive throu
philosophy and empty deception, according to the tradi
men, according to the elementary principles of the worl
than according to Christ. In Him all the fullness of Deity d
bodily form, in Him you have been made complete and He
over all rule and authority.

The most seductively dangerous area of psychology
part which seeks to explain why people are the way they a
how they change. Research says there is no success this wa
Biblical way originates with God, employs gifts and fruits
Spirit and leads a Christian into a greater awareness of Go
himself as created by God.

The psychological way originates with man, utilizes man-
techniques and ends with man. It is limited to man's assisted
effort.

The Biblical way is accomplished through God's provisi
of a new life and through His indwelling Holy Spirit, who enab
the believer to cooperate with the changes God is making wit
him. In addition, he has provided fellowship with other believe
also in the process of being transformed into the image of Jesu

The psychological way includes many theories about wh
people are the way they are and how they can change.

The Biblical way says that problems of living are due t
separation from God because of the sinful condition of mankin
and the presence of sin in the world after the fall. The Biblical answer is Jesus, who has provided the only means to reestablish a relationship between God and man and to enable people to live by faith in God.

The past belongs on the cross and under the blood of Jesus. The new life brings salvation. The old one is done away with and buried. Celebrate you, with new life in Christ.

Truly, truly, unless one is born again, he cannot see the kingdom of God. As many as received Him, He gave the right to become children of God.

The Biblical way stresses God's love, next, loving God and others. By grace you are saved. God's love is not sentimental but just and righteous. Therefore, sin has to be dealt with, and by His love, God has provided for all that each believes and needs in order to be conformed to the image of Jesus. Biblical way teaches that man is a spiritual being created in the image of God, and that man cannot find true identity apart from God. It begins and ends with the creator and sustainer of the universe. The Biblical way encourages faith in God, in his faithfulness, love, power and the word.

Psychological way encourages faith in the therapist, in his professional training and status in the psychotherapeutic theories and methodologies.

Biblical way exalts Christ. The psychological way emphasizes self. The Biblical way is God-centered; the psychological way is man-centered.

From the point of initial new life, one is choosing to walk after the Spirit (according to the new nature), rather than after the flesh (old nature). He undergoes transformation as he daily yields himself to God, choosing to walk after the Spirit. When one walks in the Spirit, he is dependent upon the Lord.

Biblical way encourages the life of the Spirit. Psychological way strengthens the flesh, treats guilt feelings, but generally avoids or dismisses the problem of sin.

The Christian can be transformed through repentance.

Another Setback: My Husband's Health Problems

It started with a small ulcer between his toes, which would not heal. He went to the wound center, and as time went by, it was decided that he must have a leg bypass, which is to take a vein from his thigh and put it in his leg. In order to do that, he had to have clearance from the heart doctor. It resulted after several tests that he would have a stint put into one of his arteries to his heart.

Lo and behold, after the stint was put into the artery, his ulcer healed. Praise God and that doctor. However, later on, an aneurysm developed, and he had to have more surgery to correct that. He is in the healing process at this time and doing well.

So here I am back to my book. It now seems to be leading to self-publish and be in control of all that is in it. God is great. Thank Him for all that He does.

Book Notes

God calls us to do for Him and we say, "Who, me? I am not qualified," etc., etc., when all is against you and we are strong enough to stand before God alone. With His strength I am led to move on with the book. The Holy Spirit spoke to me through this holy person without him knowing it.

Another person asked, "How does the book end?" I told him that it will show people that if they walk the walk and talk the talk, adhere to the word of God, then one can communicate with God. If the line is clean, not clogged with sin, one can talk to God.

God chooses the dream. God matches the dreamer to a special dream. There isn't another person who would do it as you would. God sometimes chooses the uneducated. God entrusts the dream to the dreamer. God walks away and watches you, like leaving a woman to give birth. It is up to you how you will treat it and care for it to bring it to full term. Guard it. The dream takes on a life of its own. It comes to pass at the right time. What gives the dream a life of its own? The mother. The dream keeps you going – you support the dream now, and the dream supports you. God blesses the dream. Do not block and do not abort.

Where self-esteem is concerned, do not say, "I am not the one. I am not this," etc. You can abort the dream that way. Others can discourage you, but let it come to full term. Walk the walk in faith. Only you can bring it to full term.

Again, it is all in God's timing. No matter how we try to push it, nothing develops until it is in God's timing. Patience is a virtue. Stay focused and keep the faith. God is in control, believe it.

The Thank You

In the meantime, we visited with Leilani, our lady friend, at her café and began discussing the book. She immediately grabbed Jessica's hand and said, "We are going to pray together that the book will be published."

I thank all my friends and relatives for inspiring me to move on with this book, especially my daughter Jessica, the first and foremost to give me confidence to write the book; my son, John Jr. and my daughter-in-law Diane; my brother and sister-in-law, Joseph and Lorraine Schovitz; Cathy and Linda, our friends; the Sliwka family for being my sounding board; Fran, John, and Tony, for their interest in the book; David and Julie Shadwell; also the special prayer we had with Sandy Olympio. Prayers sent out to the priests of the Sacred Heart of Jesus and the 700 Club prayer line.

Most of all, my thanks to our Lord Jesus Christ. All glory, honor and praise to God our Father.

I must add that Leilani was the prayer person, with Jessica and myself, to get it through. Real believers are a prayer powerhouse together. Time goes by; my energy is sapped. However, the inspiration goes on. As I was watching C-Span, Congressman John Kasich was speaking and said, "Follow your dreams and don't let the one close to you tell you that you can't."

A special thanks to President George Bush for the statement, "a war between good and evil."

A special thank you to the radio hostess who offered to do a radio show together. This encouraged me to carry on, even though I was not led to do it. Thanks to my brother, John Schovitz, sister Eleanor, sister Dorothy, brother-in-law Ralph, niece Marisa, who encouraged me to publish.

More thanks must go to Rita and Joe, our friends, for their interest in the book.

Marie C. Pepsin

The Forces at Work Through Certain People to Undermine My Book

First, I must say that so many have encouraged me to get it done and say that they can't wait to get the book. They are looking forward to it. They keep asking about it.

Then there is the struggle with certain other people. They have not read or seen my manuscript. Only one said, "You are not a writer." I took the remark in silence, but in my spirit something said, "When God wants to get a job done, He will work through you, no matter what you are."

Some warn of the pitfalls of publishing out there in the world.

When I mentioned about God giving me the money to get the book published, another person close to us made the remark, "You are a dreamer." He said it in a sarcastic manner.

Then there is this one individual, whom I know the devil works through. He saps me of my energy. He smirks and laughs at me when I discuss my book with someone. He makes all kinds of insulting remarks and constantly downgrades me. But, praise God, I know what is happening and know better. I'm learning to overcome him and pray each day for God to cover me with the blood of Jesus and protect me from all evil.

I must overcome all of these setbacks and continue on.

It is all in God's timing, but this book will get printed for you all to be blessed by it. God is in control. Praise Him.

As we pray about our concerns, Job 33:15-16 confirms our venture. "In a dream, in a vision of the night, when deep sleep falleth upon men, in slumberings upon the bed. Then He openeth the ears of men and sealeth their instruction." God uses dreams to protect, and God is speaking through dreams of God and visions. Dreams of the Lord, we must pray through. God impels me to take seriously what he is saying to me. Some people in the world will ridicule you, but we must stand strong.

To sum it all up, in a dream, in a vision of the night, when deep sleep falls upon us while we are in our bed, then God opens the ears of us and gives us information as we pray about our concerns.

The Struggle

It is up to you and God to follow Divine Guidance from Him and solve all that He has revealed to you. Therein lies victory. Overcome all the hurdles that come your way. He has given this all to you and He will see you through. Praise God. Just keep on going on, no matter what people say. Keep in mind the ridicule that Noah received when he was building the ark.

Note the cancer dream. The moon was part of it. The moon reflects the glory of the sun. (Son?) Pray for His protection, which is needed when you venture to give Glory and praise to our God, in the name of Jesus Christ. Jesus is Lord, Father, Son and Holy Spirit. Walk with Him. He has so much to say to you. Take time to listen. He is the way, the truth and the life, and remember, no one comes to the Father but through Him. Jesus died for our sins. Be under the covering of His blood, for therein lies your salvation, Without the blood of Jesus, you are open prey.

Notes on the Moth

One Sunday while I was praying about my book, a moth flew toward the light and settled in on the light shade.

It is not beyond plausibility that someone could confuse a hummingbird with a large moth. Remember the cancer dream? Hummingbirds are legendary in American Indian lore. In some tribes, the birds are believed to be an important symbol in the vision quest ceremony. To see a hummingbird in a dream is considered to be a time of good fortune.

Herbal moth repellent: rosemary, peppermint, thyme and cloves.

Comment about The Struggle

The Struggle is an arresting, original work that persuades any reader that the power of faith can help overcome his or her problems. At the heart of Marie C. Pepsin's book is the concept that faith and love of one's fellow man can conquer adversity.

It is recommended for publication for its unique subject matter, lucid explanation of a difficult subject and the importance of this point of view.

Readers will quickly acknowledge the author's courage, sincerity and strong faith.

Book Notes

Remember in the cancer dream, about the cutting of a cross on the lump? After my dream, I read where a woman had breast cancer and an angel came to this person. After the angel left, there was no sign of the cancer. There was just the cloth left behind on the bed, with three crosses cut in it.

Run the Race

Christ is the author and perfecter of your faith. Keep your eyes on the finish line. The goal line is Jesus Christ. God is holy, life and light.

Rituals are good for you, but throw off everything that hinders, like too much of the things that take you away from your finish line. Purify ourselves from what contaminates us.

Run the race. It will take some time to win the race, but forge on. Jesus Christ is Lord – the Father, Son and Holy Spirit. Glory and Honor is His.

Made in the USA
Charleston, SC
27 January 2017